"God's fervent love for  abused women, and *God Calls Beloved*. Elyse does an amazing job of tracing the story of God's favor towards imperfect, flawed, and broken people throughout Scripture, and I know these truths will be life-changing for many. I will be recommending this book often!"

—JOY FORREST,
founder and executive director, Called to Peace Ministries

"If anyone knows how to encourage the Christian's journey in this season of 'now, but not yet' it's Elyse Fitzpatrick. Spoiler alert, it's not meritocracy. Immerse yourself deeply into Unloved's gospel drenched biblical illustrations and then breathe because, friends, it is finished."

—ANN MAREE GOUDZWAARD,
founder and executive director, Help[H]er

"With compellingly fresh perspectives on the often overlooked and misunderstood stories of women from Scripture, Elyse invites us to take another look and see how even though they had incredibly messy lives, they were unequivocally cherished and loved by God. She encourages us to reflect on our own lives and how easy it is for us to try to wheedle out love from God by being good, but just as God loved these women, we also are his Beloved. For those who find themselves trying to earn God's affection and love, Elyse's insights offer a powerful message of God's unfailing love that will linger with you long after the final page is turned."

—PAMELA MACRAE,
professor of applied theology and church ministries,
Moody Bible Institute, Chicago, Illinois

"The stories contained in these pages exposed my soul in surprising ways. While I know I can't earn God's love, I'm not sure I recognized just how often my heart functions according to a meritocracy. I'm so thankful for Elyse's careful, winsome retelling of these stories that showed me again that I am not only deeply broken, but also deeply beloved."

—SCOTT MEHL,
pastor, Cornerstone Church of West Los Angeles, California

"*Unloved* delivers incredible reminders that my soul desperately needs. My friend Elyse has done it again, inviting all of us who feel used and cast aside to run to God's relentless love and experience freedom."

—CHRIS MOLES, pastor of The Chapel, Winfield, West Virginia;
certified counselor with the Association of Certified Biblical Counselors; author of *The Heart of Domestic Abuse*

"Elyse Fitzpatrick shares stories of how God's undeserving people have experienced the richness of his everlasting love, found only in Christ. What a breath of fresh air! Read this for your own heart and share it with a friend."

—SHAUNA VAN DYKE,
founder and biblical counselor, Truth Renewed Ministries;
strategic advisor, The Association of Biblical Counselors (ABC)

"Elyse has gifted us with a long lingering look at the unfailing love and value God demonstrates for those we might label unlovable, unattractive, unsuccessful, undeserving, and unwanted. If you've ever struggled with the 'I'm not _____ enough' syndrome, this book is for you. You don't have to be good enough, smart enough, or spiritual enough to be wildly loved by a good and generous God."

—LESLIE VERNICK,
Christian counselor; international speaker; relationship coach;
author of *The Emotionally Destructive Relationship*
and *The Emotionally Destructive Marriage*

Unloved

The Rejected Saints God Calls Beloved

Unloved

The Rejected Saints God Calls Beloved

Elyse M. Fitzpatrick

LEXHAM PRESS

Unloved: The Rejected Saints God Calls Beloved

Copyright 2025 Elyse Fitzpatrick

Lexham Press, 1313 Commercial St., Bellingham, WA 98225
LexhamPress.com

You may use brief quotations from this resource in presentations, articles, and books. For all other uses, please write Lexham Press for permission. Email us at permissions@lexhampress.com.

Unless otherwise noted, Scripture quotations are from the Christian Standard Bible®, Copyright © 2017 by Holman Bible Publishers. Used by permission. Christian Standard Bible, and CSB® are federally registered trademarks of Holman Bible Publishers.

Scripture quotations marked (NIV) are from the Holy Bible, NEW INTERNATIONAL VERSION®. Copyright © 1973, 1978, 1984, 2011 by Biblica, Inc. Used by permission. All rights reserved worldwide.

Scripture quotations marked (NLT) are from the Holy Bible, New Living Translation, copyright © 1996, 2004, 2007, 2013 by Tyndale House Foundation. Used by permission of Tyndale House Publishers, Inc., Carol Stream, Illinois 60188. All rights reserved.

Print ISBN 9781683597827
Digital ISBN 9781683597834
Library of Congress Control Number 2024944037

Lexham Editorial: Rachel Joy Welcher, Claire Brubaker, Mandi Newell
Cover Design: Jonathan Myers
Typesetting: Abigail Stocker

24 25 26 27 28 29 30 / US / 12 11 10 9 8 7 6 5 4 3 2 1

*To all the women and men who have been crushed
by the Law, look at the problems in their lives
and wonder whether they're loved or not.
You are free. You are Beloved. Hang on.*

Contents

Introduction 1

1: Two Stories 9
2: An Unbelievable Parable 25
3: Too Wonderful to Believe 41
4: Beloved Outcasts, Hagar and Photine 59
5: Tamar and Judah 79
6: Finding Refuge under His Wings 97
7: David and Bathsheba 113
8: And Yet 133

Epilogue 149
Appendix: How to Know You Are a Christian 155
Endnotes 161
Bibliography 163

Introduction

In *Free of Charge*, Croatian theologian Miroslav Volf rightly identifies the kind of god whom many Christians mistakenly worship. He identifies him as either the Negotiator or the Gift Giver. Volf describes the Negotiator as a god who makes deals, while the Gift Giver is like Santa, one who disperses gifts willy-nilly, regardless of what a person might actually need. The Negotiator and the Gift Giver sadly resemble the view many of us have of God. But this misunderstanding is nothing new. Ever since Adam and Eve first lost their open and free relationship with God and learned to cry, they and their descendants have vainly sought to rediscover life and relationship with him. Shamed exiles, they wandered in the dark, constructing false versions of God, futilely trying to find their way back to intimacy with him.

Their loss is our loss, too. We have also misunderstood the Lord and turned him into a god we can comprehend and control. We've judged him by our success or failure. We've tried to buy our way back to Eden through our good works and diligent effort. We've thought it a good idea to try to make deals with him or cajole him into giving us the sweets we crave, while all along the Savior calls us to come home to him and trust in his love.

Tragically, I've found Volf's diagnosis all too true. Too many who would identify as followers of Jesus have been taught that, in order to be blessed, they need to imitate the heroes of the Bible: Sarah, Abraham, Moses, David, Esther, and Peter. They have been taught that these legendary Bible characters received blessings from God because they earned them or because they were the sort of people God could be proud of. This has led many believers to try to ingratiate themselves to God through their own works so that they too can assure themselves that they deserve blessings. They have been taught that God is, in Volf's words, a Negotiator. This way of thinking turns the Christian life into a nonstop foxhole conversion prayer: *If you get me out of this mess, or give me this thing I want, or bless me the way I want to be blessed, I will do thus-and-so for you.* Or a game of give-and-take: *Since I've done this good thing for you, it's time for my reward!* Of course, the ultimate problem with these negotiations is that God doesn't need anything from us. As the apostle Paul asks, "Who has ever given to God, that he should be repaid?" (Romans 11:35). God doesn't need our faith or obedience or sacrifice. He owns the cattle on a thousand hills (Psalm 50) and refuses to negotiate in any sort of quid pro quo arrangement. He needs nothing. He can't be bought. He doesn't make deals. He owes no debt.

Neither is God a Santa figure—the jolly old grandpa who gives children too much sugar just because he likes to see them smile at his generosity. This doesn't mean that God is stingy. It means that the gifts he gives are always for our good because he loves us, not because he is trying to buy our love by filling our trick-or-treat bag with full-size Reese's Peanut Butter Cups (dark chocolate, of course). While it is true that God is scandalously generous, he is also truly loving, which means that he will give gifts only that result in our eternal benefit. This truth is most clearly illustrated in his inexpressible gift of his Son, Jesus Christ. God's gifts are just that, *gifts*—not a wage to be earned by cozying up to good old gramps.

Good and Gracious God

Within this book, you will find the stories of women and men whose lives would be best characterized by the word "messy." None of them were consistently faithful, loving, kind, or courageous. They were weak and sinful. If the Lord were the Negotiator God, every one of them would have failed miserably to uphold their part of the deal. If he were the Gift-Giving Grandpa God, they would have consumed all the candy and spent their lives in agony on the bathroom floor. And most of them would never have even stopped to murmur a bloated, "Thank you."

And yet, even though they often failed, constantly misunderstood their calling, wronged and abused one another, mistrusted God, broke their word, and wasted so many of the good gifts they were given, they are still—miraculously—called God's beloved. On their own, they deserved the name "unloved"—they were destitute before God. In addition, most of them never stopped to realize that any blessings they enjoyed were pure gifts from God for which they should have been grateful. Instead, they vacillated between viewing themselves as unlovable losers or virtuous overachievers, neither of which matches God's description of who we are in him.

It should not surprise us that women and men in ancient times—before the Scriptures were canonized and the gospel was clearly proclaimed—misinterpreted their identity, their purpose, and their God despite his continually seeking them (see Acts 17:27). Many of the people discussed in this book had only a dim light, and yet, in their desperate faith, they did try to reach out and find him. They knew they needed a rescuer but couldn't imagine what he would be like. They lived their entire lives in twilight, with only a few angelic visitations, visions, or fragments of truth. As Hebrews 11:13 says, "They did not receive the things promised; they only saw them and welcomed them from a distance" (NIV). Even after the nation of Israel was called out of Egypt and Moses had told them of God's commands, virtually none had held a copy of God's word in their own hands. Others made it into the land of promise but still had to fight continually to survive. They were bereft exiles, wandering in gloom.

Even so, the ancients walked by faith in ways that we supposedly enlightened moderns just can't fathom. Even though they failed miserably, they were still beloved. They were God's backward children, trying to do what they thought was right to appease God, to survive, hoping to earn some sort of a blessed life. In his great condescension, the Lord revealed himself to them in ways that they would be able to accept, and he continued to uphold them and weave their story into his. Because he loved and understood them, he gently spoke baby talk to them, continually wooing them to himself so that they would be assured that he was their God and they were his people. And still they wandered.

Which brings us to a conundrum: we've been given so much more than they had. Most of us have multiple copies of the Scriptures in our homes. We have the Holy Spirit, comforting us and working through us to live the Christian life. We have constant reminders of our salvation in the sacraments, and we have the fellowship of the church. Most importantly, we have the example of Jesus Christ, who took on flesh and dwelt among us. He was the physical, living revelation of God to us (see Hebrews 1:1–3).

Everything we need in order to walk in the light in deep communion with him is ours. So, why do so many of us continue to misinterpret God's nature? Why do we think he wants to barter with us? Why do we work to try to earn his blessing? Why do we think we can obligate him? Why do we judge his love for us by whether our lives are Instagram-able or not? Why do we doubt that we are really beloved? Hasn't he given us the truth we need? Hasn't he sent his Son to show us who he is and make the way for us to return to him?

In the pages that follow, you will be introduced (or possibly reintroduced) to women and men whose lives were just like ours. The difference, of course, is that we are living on this side of Bethlehem, Calvary, and Pentecost. Their lives will serve to instruct and encourage us. But they will also rebuke us because we have been given so much more than they were and yet we still struggle to believe that God loves us generously, lavishly, and by his own choice. We are still confused about who he is.

For those of us privileged to lead others into a deeper understanding of God's love, I pray this book will remind you to remind them that it may appear that they are unloved, but if they have trusted in Christ, they are beloved by him. Nothing can ever change that. No matter how things look today, they are loved because God chooses to love them. If they are in the Beloved Son (Ephesians 1:6), the Father loves them like family (John 17:23). The same love the Father has for the Son is theirs. Now. Today. Always. Remind them of these truths.

Quick Housekeeping Notes

Two items before we get started: I write with the assumption that my reader is someone who has already committed their life to Christ. What I mean by that is that you have transferred your trust from your own ability to earn God's love and onto Jesus as the only one perfect enough to please God and earn the name Beloved. If you haven't done that yet, or if you are unsure how to, please turn to appendix 1 now, where you will learn more about this life of faith.

Second, at the end of every chapter, you will find a series of questions that are meant to help you think through what you have just read. At the end of these questions, I have included an encouragement to summarize what you learned in the chapter. Personally, I've found this to be a helpful exercise. Here's why: Did you ever recommend a book but, when asked about its contents, struggled to explain exactly why it helped you?

The exercise of summarizing forces me to organize what I have learned and also provides me with a resource to return to in the future. Knowing ahead of time that I'll need to summarize what I'm reading also helps me take note of what's there.

Now, here's my prayer for us as we begin this journey together:

> Father, please grant us faith to believe the love you have so generously and freely promised in Ephesians 3:17–20. Please help us believe that our lives will continue to be nourished and sustained by your overwhelming love, no matter how we look to ourselves or to others. Grant us the ability to grow in our understanding of your love, and give us an ever-expanding vision of your unfathomable compassion and care for us, all to the end that we will be willing to open every part of our hearts and lives to you. Free us from any faulty beliefs about who you are or how you relate to us as anything other than your children. Transform our thinking away from any foolishness about how we can earn what you have already given. You can do this because you've called us your own beloved children and because you are able to do far more than we could ever ask or think. Glorify yourself through us, we pray, in Jesus's name. Amen.

Now, here's my hope for us as we begin this journey together: I hope that you will walk away from this book with a new freedom and a new joy. I pray that you will be freed from the idea that you must earn love from a Negotiator God who sells blessings to wage earners, or from any silliness about God's senility. And I pray that your joy will be renewed as you see how much he loves all who audaciously trust that he is trustworthy, believing that he will always give each of us what is best. Why? Because he loves to call unloved messes his beloved children.

1

Two Stories

Over the last fifty years, I have had far too many conversations with fellow believers that could be summed up in the question, "Am I loved?" The sad truth is that many Christians don't know for sure. Their lives don't seem to line up with the life they imagined for themselves when they came to faith. As a result, they question what they have believed about God, and frequently their suffering speaks louder to them than the Bible.

Maybe this questioning flows from a childhood where parents were absent, critical, or cold. Perhaps it stems from adult relationships (or lack of them): friends who betrayed them, family members who abused them, employers who denigrated them, or churches that deceived them. Or perhaps they are, by nature, people who simply have trouble believing they are worthy of love. Some of us are so self-critical, so introspective, that it doesn't matter how many people tell us they love us; it's never enough. We incessantly wonder, *Am I loved?* And we don't seem to hear God's resounding answer: yes.

To make matters worse, some of us have been taught that our desire to be loved should be ignored. We have wrongly believed that our longing to feel loved is actually a temptation to be resisted. I have heard and believed this teaching myself—in fact, I have even been the one to teach it. Before I wrote *Because He Loves Me*, I thought that focusing on God's love was something that immature believers did. Truly "mature" Christians didn't need to hear about God's love. Rather, they needed to focus on the ways they either succeeded or failed to love God as they should. *My* love for God was what mattered. Many have been taught that a relationship with God is reciprocal, like the one you have with your employer: you put in a good day's work, and your employer responds by giving you a raise, or at least by not firing you. While this is true in the workaday world, it's antithetical to God's kingdom.

Sadly, messages like this abound in Christian media—messages that insist that God keeps track of whether you're naughty or nice—and they turn the suffering Christ, dying for ungrateful sinners, into the not-so-jolly man from the north who has sent out a legion of elves to judge your worthiness. The message of the suffering servant will never appeal to those who punctiliously keep the rules so they can earn blessing. There's nothing more insulting or infuriating to the smugly religious person than to discover that their good works earn nothing, while an audacious whore finds the gates of heaven flung open wide as she covers Christ's filthy feet with kisses and tears. Too many pretend followers of Jesus would find the company he kept shameful. And when he refused to enter into any political power scheme because his kingdom was not of this world, they would have gone screaming from the room. To suggest that God demands to be known as the one who loves sinners and reserves his harshest criticism for those who think they can earn his blessing was, and is, for many a bridge too far. He refuses to be the Negotiator God who welcomes those who think they need just a dab of goodness here or there.

In spite of the fact that the Lord has proclaimed his love for the unlovely, we're surprised when we open the Bible and find story after story of unfaithful, scheming losers called beloved, blessed, and chosen. In the pages that follow, you'll discover stories of unloving husbands, devious wives, unbelieving believers, proud beggars, ungrateful receivers, and those whose lives are just like our own: stories of people who longed to be loved and, despite all odds and in spite of their failure, were loved beyond their wildest imaginations.

God Is Love

Let me tell you what I know about you: you were made to love and to be loved. How do I know that? Because I know the One who formed you. In the same way we resemble our parents, God our Father made us in his image. His spiritual DNA saturates our soul because we were made to be like him (see Genesis 1:26). And what is God like? He is *love* (1 John 4:8). Think of that. The very essence of the one who created you is *love*. That is why I know that you were made to love and be loved, to be beloved.

We can't help but long for loving relationships. Every story we read, every life lived, is shaped by this desire to be the beloved.

Think for a moment about the main character in your favorite novel. Whether Jean Valjean in *Les Misérables* or Harry in *Harry Potter*, each is, in their own way, looking to be loved. What drives their stories? Love is the reason behind everything we do. Our contentment, happiness, and peace all rest on whether we believe that we are loved. Sure, we want to be respected. We want to know that we are useful and accomplishing something worthwhile. Yes, we long to know that we have significance in the eyes of those we value and that they will continue to be committed to us because we're getting it done. But all those desires are really rooted in this overriding one: for love. We are people created for love. Love is at our core. We want to know we are worthy of love. And we want to love other worthy people in return. We want to be beloved.

Because we have been made like the God who defines himself as love, the knowledge that we are loved has the power to determine whether we live a life that is ultimately satisfying and rewarding or empty and miserable. No one can live a happy life in complete isolation, which is why not even the most introverted among us truly wishes to be a shipwrecked castaway or a prisoner condemned to solitary confinement. We were created *in* love, *for* love.

Even so, the sad reality is that many Christians feel unloved. They look at their lives, the ways they have failed or the ways that others have failed them, and they are sure that whatever a life of love might look like, this couldn't possibly be it. Sure, God might love people, and maybe he even created them for love, but that's not a story that applies to them. Perhaps they're convinced that they're just not good enough to be worthy of love. They don't make the grade. Thoughts like *I've done THAT THING way too many times*, or *I did that ONE REALLY TERRIBLE thing*, are on auto-play in their hearts. They are convinced that they are not worthy of anyone's love, and especially not God's. Or perhaps the pain they have experienced stripped them of any faith they might have had before the darkness closed in.

You might think, If there actually is a God and if he's supposed to be good, wise, powerful, and loving, then why does every breath I take have to hurt so much? Is he sadistic? Weak? Stupid? And, of course, if you can't bring yourself to think those thoughts about the Lord, then the obvious conclusion must be that you're the problem. There must be something intrinsically wrong with you, some bentness that God isn't able to straighten. Or perhaps—worse yet—he just doesn't want to. You're not worth his time. Maybe God is so cruel that he made you for love but refused to make you lovable.

Christianity Is Not a Meritocracy

Sometimes we have trouble believing we are loved because we haven't understood God's grace. Instead, we've heard that God's kingdom is a meritocracy. A meritocracy is a place where we earn a wonderful life by our own ability, work, or goodness. In a meritocracy, we earn love and the life we want by what we do and who we are. God is like a cosmic vending machine. We drop in our obedience, good deeds, hard work, and religious busyness, and a life filled with love, richness, and blessing magically appears in exchange. These strategies are everywhere in the church: in sermons, Sunday school, and Christian conferences. But as you'll see in this book, that's nothing new.

Being able to earn a great life might sound like good news, but it isn't. Why? Because it puts us in an impossible position. We're deceived into thinking that if we just try hard enough, believe that we're good enough, and never, ever, give up, we can earn all the goodies we long for. But that responsibility is doomed to failure; it will ultimately crush us. Jesus's shoulders are the only ones broad enough to carry the demands of a meritocracy, and it killed him. But he rose again. For us.

In wealthy contexts, like the one I live in, in twenty-first-century Southern California, blessing in a meritocracy looks like having a nice family, a nice house (with a view), and a nice car. It looks like good health and plenty of money at the end of the month to go out to whatever restaurant happens to be popular at the time. It looks like success in all your endeavors (especially the ones for the Lord) and loads of friends and followers on social media. It looks like a good reputation and knowing that you're leaving a praiseworthy legacy.

How do I get this life I'm longing for? Simple. I need to believe that I can do it and then give myself a pep talk whenever I feel like giving up. I need to not buy into any negativity about my limitations or failure. Faith is believing I can do it—be successful, powerful, happy—and refusing to listen to any lies about how life is beyond my control. Faith in myself and my tenacity is what will bless me.

This perspective appeals to me because I hate to admit that I'm not powerful or in control. In a meritocracy, the only thing that is considered a sin is the acceptance of failure. *If I can just muster up enough faith in myself, then my life will surely be blessed. I need to believe that I have the power to justify myself and prove that I'm okay after all* are the thoughts that propel life in a meritocracy.

Meritocracy Lite

In this lite perspective, God doesn't ask a lot of you. He's the gift-giving grandpa. What he asks is pretty easily accomplished by keeping a tidy house, not whining all the time, and never, ever thinking negative thoughts about yourself. He really likes seeing you happy, and so he'll give you all the treats you might want, no matter whether they're good for you or not.

I realize that meritocracy lite also seems like good news, but it actually isn't because it teaches you to look to yourself for blessings. How are you doing at keeping the house tidy? How many days has it been since you complained? Did you remember to pack your kids' lunches with nothing but healthy choices? Did you cut out their sandwiches in the shape of hearts? Did you banish every thought that you might not be as wonderful as your grandpa said? Listen, if other people can be great, so can you. Right? Just believe in yourself.

Meritocracy Heavy

I assume that some of you are like me, and you shake your head in annoyance at such silliness. You might even find yourself being agitated that some people have the audacity to call meritocracy lite "Christianity." I know that there was a time in my life when I would have felt that way, too. I told myself that the Christianity I had embraced was based on the *Bible* and not *feelings*. It certainly wasn't founded on faith in myself or the pursuit of superficial worldly pleasures. Or was it? My Christianity was all about strict obedience. And while striving to be obedient is not wrong, for many of us, it leads to believing that God is obligated to bless us.

By the way, you can test whether you have inadvertently bought into this thinking by how you respond when you're faced with unexpected trials or hardship. Faced with sudden financial shortfall? An unwelcome medical diagnosis? The loss of a relationship? If these trials cause you to automatically go inward and begin questioning what you've done to disappoint God, you are living under the demands of a meritocracy. I once talked with a friend who told me that she had a difficult day because she had neglected to read her Bible and pray that morning. While I find it easy to dismiss this kind of thinking, I recognize that my faith is far more transactional than I care to admit. When things go wrong in your life, what are the questions you ask yourself?

Sadly, much of what passes for serious Christianity has more to do with merit-based systems of non-Christian cults than the faith Paul lived and died for. If Christianity actually is a way to earn blessings from God, then it wouldn't have gotten the apostles martyred. Meritocracy heavy, being ultra-committed to obedience to the law, is alluring because all of us want to believe that we can do it. Even though I might scoff at meritocracy lite, at its core this heavy version is no different. I'm still tempted to believe that I can save myself by my own determination to trust and obey.

Living in either version of a meritocracy might not seem so bad at first. We think good works = good life. But this scheme never pans out the way we think it will. This is because none of us can ever be good enough to obligate God. Why not? Because God is perfect and demands perfection (Matthew 5:48). In fact, James 2:10 says that if we break just one part of God's law, we are guilty of breaking it all. None of us has ever obeyed perfectly—not as we should have. We consistently fail to love God and our neighbor. Even on the good days when we think we're nailing it, we easily fall into sin: *Look at me!* we think. *I was kind to the barista who got my order wrong!* Right then, we've fallen into pride and self-worship. We are always just one step away from judging others who aren't quite as worthy as we are. No, a meritocracy isn't good news for sinners. In fact, it's terrifying.

Considering this brokenness, we must accept that we are unable to earn anything from God. Ever. Although this might not look like good news, it is actually the best news we could ever hear. That's because, if we let it, it will destroy all our self-trust and force us to free-fall onto the mercy of God, the only place where sinners can find rest. There we will learn what it means to be justified: to be completely forgiven *and* to be counted perfectly obedient. Without any sin to condemn us, we can find rest in the perfect record of Jesus, the only one good enough to actually earn blessing in a meritocracy. He perfectly obeyed every part of the law in our place. He earned every true blessing we desire. So, maybe God's kingdom really is a meritocracy after all: one where Jesus earned our merit and then died for our demerit.

Jesus not only earned all the blessings; he also paid for all the failures. He lived perfectly *in our place*, died shamefully *in our place*, rose bodily *in our place*, and is seated in heaven as our Savior right now, overseeing everything in our life. That's the message of the gospel, a word that means "good news." The good news is that you and I can rely on a perfect person to be perfect in our place. Everything that needed to be done to deserve God's blessing has already been done. All we have to do now is believe the gospel, believe that someone already loves us, no matter how we've failed. We are already completely, fully, and utterly beloved. All the earning and payment needed has already been resolved. The Judge has pronounced us not guilty. In addition, a meritocracy has been satisfied. We are not only not guilty; we are also perfect law-keepers. We have all the merit we need to receive God's benediction of "beloved one." Why? Because we now wear the righteousness of Jesus.

The Bad News

As you can see, the thought that you can obligate God to bless you is not only frustrating; it's impossible. This false message says that God's love for you is based on your faith or work for him. It drives you to seek to justify yourself, and it's the underlying message in a recent tweet I stumbled on that said, "If you start by being thankful for small things, you will soon have big things to be thankful for!" What is the underlying message here? You're the one who determines whether big things are coming your way. Here's another: "You're going to see what your parents and grandparents dreamed of. You're going to walk in the blessing that they prayed for. Because they honored God, ancient gates are about to open for you. You're going to see generational blessings." What's the message here? It's that your parents and grandparents earned blessings for you. They earned the merit that you needed to enjoy that blessed life of love you have always longed for. With a perspective like this, when your life doesn't look the way you hoped it would, perhaps you can blame your parents. Or your grandparents. They didn't pray enough or believe enough or work hard enough. That leaves you in the terrible position of trying to dig your way out of a hole. How will you ever make up for their failures and earn what you long for from God?

I would imagine that for most of my readers, these messages are obviously false. But perhaps you've heard other ones that aren't quite so blatantly wrong. See if you can discern what's wrong with them:

> As a woman, if you dress modestly, God will give you a faithful husband.

> If you are sexually pure before marriage, God will give you a sexually satisfying married life.

> If you read your Bible and pray every day, God will make all your days sing.

> If you follow prescribed gender roles in marriage, your spouse will love you the way you want to be loved.
>
> If you homeschool your children, they will grow up to be faithful Christians.
>
> If you attend church faithfully, God will furnish you with answers and support.

Can you hear the underlying message? Perhaps those statements aren't as obviously false as the ones I quoted above, but at their heart they contain the same erroneous theology. They say that you can control your future and assure yourself of a blessed life through your own actions. Any time you hear an *if-then* message about your relationship with the Lord, alarm bells should go off.

Now, I'm not saying that we should be immodest, promiscuous, lazy, or disobedient to what we believe God is asking of us, uninvolved in the training of our children, or detached from other believers. Not at all. What I am saying is that God's gracious generosity to us is not based on our work at all; the lives we're called to live won't determine whether we'll have the kind of life we're hoping for. Our relationship with God is based solely on the work of Jesus Christ. Each of our days rests in the hands of a sovereign, loving God. All the earning has already been done.

You and I have been invited into a story. It's the story of someone who silenced the demands of a meritocracy by his perfect obedience and substitutionary death for us, the unworthy. He has loved the unlovable. He laid down his life—not for those who deserve it but for those who couldn't have cared less (see Romans 5:8). He did this for those who weren't good parents, who weren't humble and obedient, who were instead demanding, immodest, and unfaithful. In other words, he did it for us! He entered into everything we have earned: punishment, judgment, and condemnation.

Certainly, if Jesus knew that we had to pay our way into relationship with him, he would have abandoned us long ago. But he didn't because we don't. Not only that, but his obedience was perfect, and yet he chose to suffer in our place. So, we are free to turn from the bad news spewed out in a meritocracy and throw ourselves fully onto the mercy of God, whose Son earned all the merit required. God has transferred all that merit, blessing, and love to us in his Son—freely and fully, forever.

We Were Made for Love

Once again, a major part of what it means to be made in God's image and to live as his representatives is to give and receive love. His entire will for our lives can be summed up in just two commands, both centered on love: we are to love him and love others (see Matthew 22:37–39). But here's the rub: love for others can't be forced on demand, no matter how hard we try. It flows from only one place: the knowledge that we ourselves are loved. John writes, "We love *because* he first loved us" (1 John 4:19). That's why it's *so* important for us to get this right: we are loved because of what he's done, not because we've earned it.

No matter how many times we read that we're loved or how dearly Jesus paid to prove it, many of us still struggle to believe. And this unbelief does seem reasonable, considering

Paul's description in Titus 3:3: "For we too were once foolish, disobedient, deceived, enslaved by various passions and pleasures, living in malice and envy, hateful, detesting one another." Wow. Look at that description again: full of "malice," "hateful," "detesting one another." If that's God's verdict, how dare we assume we're beloved? Thankfully, Paul goes on to write, "But when the kindness of God our Savior and his love for mankind appeared, he saved us—not by works of righteousness that we had done, but according to his mercy" (Titus 3:4–5). We are saved from his just judgment. Yes, we are unloving lawbreakers who deserve condemnation. But his salvation reaches down into our self-loathing and sets us free from guilt and shame. Because we know that we are loved even in our failure, we can be honest with ourselves. We can admit that we aren't, even now, what we should be. Yet, we can also have confidence and hope. We are both truly known and deeply loved. We are beloved because we are *his*, and he is kind, merciful, and most of all compassionate.

In the chapters to come, you will be reminded of the stories of women and men who were loved while their lives frequently looked like train wrecks. You'll recognize their struggle to earn blessings in a meritocracy and how they walked in both unbelief and faith. You'll probably see a lot of yourself in them. I certainly saw myself as I considered their stories. Many of them were working hard to try to earn their way, and yet God blessed them in spite of their failures. the Lord's love is everlasting and reaches each of us, even the messiest.

Digging Deeper

1. The apostle John writes that "God is love" (1 John 4:8). Do you believe this? More particularly, do you believe that he loves you personally? Why or why not?

2. What is a meritocracy? What are the differences between the lite and heavy versions? Where do you see yourself?

3. What's the problem with thinking that Christianity is a meritocracy? Why is this actually bad news?

4. What is the good news?

5. Summarize what you've learned in this chapter in four or five sentences.

2

An Unbelievable Parable

Do you remember flannelgraphs? They were props used to illustrate Bible stories in the days before videos and streaming services. I remember seeing some stories about Jesus walking on the water when I was a child attending Sunday school. A drawing of the water was placed on a cloth-covered board, and then the teacher would take a felt Jesus figure and move him along, above the water line. Then, of course, Peter would get out of the boat and go crashing under the waves. Later, when I became a Christian (fifty-plus years ago), I, too, would teach Bible stories using those same props. Imagine paper dolls with fuzzy material on the back that could stick to an upright board covered in flannel (Google it, if you must).

Certain Bible stories lend themselves easily to those sweetly simplistic methods, especially in a meritocracy. Noah and the ark, David and Goliath, or Daniel in the lion's den worked really well. But the truth is that the Bible isn't a children's story (though children can understand it, oftentimes better than adults!). The Scriptures were written for women and men, many of them desperate and completely lost in ancient and frequently very brutal civilizations. Their lives were not tidy. They had to fight every day to stay alive, and their relationship with the many deities was terrifying. They consistently tried to appease the earth, weather, and fertility gods, and the means they used to do so were frequently violent and bloody. Even those stories that seemed to fit nicely on flannelgraphs were actually pretty brutal. Noah's flood, Goliath's decapitated head, and political prisoners being fed to hungry lions testified to a world filled with death and destruction. When told in full detail, not one of them reads like a Hallmark card.

In fact, there are a number of R-rated stories that, if written in a modern novel, you probably wouldn't let your kids read. Here's one: in order for the people of Israel to get over their belief in their own goodness, the Lord told his prophet Hosea to marry a prostitute. Yes, you read that right. We would be wrong to assume that she was merely a woman who had a checkered past, who had become the poster child for a reformed life of purity. No. She was still a prostitute when Hosea married her. The book of Hosea in the Old Testament tells this story. Why would God ask this of his faithful prophet? It was so that his people and those in future generations, including us, would be able to see a clear picture of redemptive love and be forever freed from thinking we must earn his love through our goodness.

Hosea's relationship with his immoral wife, Gomer, wasn't a sweet flannelgraph Sunday school lesson. It was a living parable about God's scandalous love for scandalous people like us. God wants his daughters and sons to know who they are and who he is. He is the faithful, loving husband to an undeserving bride. In their idolatry, Hosea's people had been playing the role of an adulterous wife who continued to return to the slavery of prostitution instead of accepting the love of a faithful, forgiving husband. But God did not only want his people to see themselves and their sin in the person of Gomer. He wanted them to see his love in the person of Hosea, a man who loved the unlovely and forgave the unforgivable. God's love is meant to change our identity—how we think about ourselves and those around us. One of the ways he transforms us is by giving us a new name.

Who You Are because of Who I Am

I've never been crazy about my name, especially when I was young and was mistakenly called Elsie on the first day each new school year. I cringed because those were the days when a certain dairy advertised their mascot, Elsie the Cow, on television. And yes, I was a chubby child. So, "the cow" fit a little too perfectly. I'm sure that the name Elsie is lovely now that no one knows about the cow. It was just a bad time for me. And yes, I like my name now—it made it easy to set up a website.

But imagine growing up with a name that means "no love." Imagine knowing that the only reason you're alive is that God wanted to use your family to show how unfaithful your nation was, so he told your dad, a righteous prophet, to defile himself by marrying your mother, a whore. Imagine having a brother whose name told of the crushing of your country, and another brother whose name meant that God was going to abandon his people and leave them fatherless.

Gomer, the prostitute, became the mother of a daughter whom the Lord named Lo-ruhamah, which meant "no love" or "no compassion." Gomer's daughter would be a living rebuke to the unfaithful nation and to also her unfaithful mother. Gomer was a woman who, for whatever reason, had never been transformed by God's love. It would be easy to think that the reason she wouldn't welcome faithful, gracious love was that she enjoyed being a prostitute, but I doubt it. No dearly loved little girl ever says, "When I grow up I hope I get to be a hooker." No. Women who denigrate their bodies in this way usually do so because they see no other option or because they think that is what they deserve. Perhaps Gomer was an orphan with no father to protect her. Maybe she was a widow and had nothing to live on. Maybe she just needed food. Or perhaps she just liked being able to say, "I do what I want." Gomer may have been a person who justified herself through her rebellious choices. So, she made a choice that soon became a lifestyle. In fact, even when she was finally in a place of security with husband and family, she had so defined herself as unloved that she couldn't believe anything different. So, back to prostitution and self-degradation she went, even though she no longer needed to. Giving up the destructive and foolish ways we may have used to show that we are free to do whatever we want is really hard. Turning from self-destructive habits toward a life that welcomes and rests in the Lord's love may take a lifetime. Sometimes, we never know complete release from them. It appears that Gomer didn't.

In some ways, I'm like her. I know that I'm loved by God and forgiven, and yet sometimes I still fail to believe it. I go back to my old ways of making myself feel loved and justified. I don't resort to prostitution, but I eat or drink or watch or complain or judge or speak in ways that resemble my old identity instead of who I know God has called me to be in Christ. I admit that, some days, I fail to believe that what he has said about me is actually true. On those days, I feel like I must fight for what I think I need, or somehow prove that I am not what I once was. My identity as Lo-ruhamah, my former self, still has roots deep in my soul. Do you see that in yourself as well? Do you ever feel like you have something to prove? Do you ever feel like you must earn God's love? If so, you're still operating under that old name and that worthless scheme.

No one wants to admit they are Gomer, Lo-ruhamah, or her brothers. But what if the only way to know you're truly loved is to embrace this truth about yourself? What if the only way to be beloved is to say, "I don't deserve love and yet he calls me his beloved?" What if God, in his sovereign grace, chooses to use your brokenness and unbelief as a parable about the gracious love he has for you and for our broken race? What if he means for us to see that we are just like Gomer? Are we willing to be the broken ones? Are we willing to declare his unfailing love from our place in the dust? God used Hosea's story to speak to Israel about his love for them. He also uses it to declare joyous news to millions of people who see themselves as troubled, as abandoned, as unloved, and yet are told, "I've taken all your trouble onto myself. I've adopted you. You are beloved."

It's for the Kingdom

Many people think that the way to convince others to become Christians is by looking put-together, prosperous, successful, smart, and victorious. We believe that if we work hard enough, we will receive the blessings that we long for, and those blessings will make the message of the gospel look more attractive.

It's easy to assume that the reason the rise in the percentage of those who have turned from religion, the "nones" (those with no religious affiliation), the reason for the rise of the "ex-vangelicals," is that we're not projecting enough success or power. But that would be a mistake. Jesus's message is not "Work more, try harder." His message is, "You're broken. Come to me and I'll make you well." Instead, we hear and repeat this falsehood: "You could use a little help. Come to me and I'll show you how to make yourself better." Yes, the ex-vangelical/none movement is growing. But it isn't because Jesus or the gospel message has let people down. It's because our message has been the bad news of a meritocracy. And who would want that?

This mistake we're making is nothing new. It was demonstrated long ago in the disciples' continual desire to be first, to crush the Romans, and to be the ones inaugurating the kingdom. They silenced mothers who hoped God would bless their children (Mark 10:13). They wanted to punish any who didn't openly welcome them (Luke 9:54) or weren't part of their in-group (Mark 9:38–41). It's why they wanted to chastise people who weren't exactly like them, and it's why they wanted to silence beggars who cried out for mercy (see Matthew 20:30; Mark 10:46–48). And, most importantly, it made them utterly deaf to Jesus's frequent warnings about his upcoming execution. Thomas couldn't see the Father in the Son because he had his own version of what the Messiah's success would look like, and it wasn't a shamed criminal with bloody wounds. Peter had faith in his own faith and assumed that he was up for whatever might be coming his way. He soon found himself staring into the eyes of the one he had betrayed (Luke 22:61). Yet, instead of condemnation and hatred, Jesus's eyes were filled with love and understanding. Peter made it because, and only because, Jesus loved and prayed for him.

Jesus knows who we are. He knew who Hosea was. He knew why the old life called so strongly to Gomer and how she failed to believe that she was the one he was loving and would continue to love. He knew the plans he had for her children despite the seeming failure of Hosea's ministry. Who wouldn't have shaken their head in disgust when they heard that Hosea had *once again* brought that woman back into his home?

Jesus knew that millions of people who were promised love struggled to believe it. Instead they tried to assure themselves of their worthiness by their successes, and he continued to call them his beloved. He calls you beloved, too, no matter how many times you have tried and failed to merit his grace.

The Lord's Declaration

In Hosea's prophecies, Gomer is the perfect example of a person who flunked out of a meritocracy. Even though she was given love, she continued to squander it. She had been chosen to portray God's affection for sinners, but her sinful reality continued to define her, even when the possibility of a new life—a restored reputation—was offered. Her children were named after her and Israel's failures. The very thing she would have taken pride in, her children, was what continued to declare her legacy of failure. And while it's true that they had the names they deserved, the Lord shockingly announced, "I will have compassion on her," and "I will make them my own" (see Hosea 2:23). Despite Gomer's unfaithfulness, the Lord loved her deeply. He had mercy on her. She and her whole family were God's *unloved beloved*.

Even though God had graciously chosen Israel as his special people, those on whom he would pour out blessings, they consistently put their trust in themselves. They thought they could earn a better life by worshiping other gods. The truth is, they refused Yahweh's gracious offer of love and pursued their desired blessings "under every green tree" (Jeremiah 2:20).

From Hosea's living parable, we see that people who deserve God's just judgment are lavished with mercy instead. In this book, over and over again, we hear of God's lament and judgment for abandoning him, and yet we also hear heartbreaking and heart-reassuring words of promised grace and compassion:

- "I am going to persuade her, lead her to the wilderness, and speak tenderly to her" (Hosea 2:14).

- "I will take you to be my wife forever. I will take you to be my wife in righteousness, justice, love, and compassion. I will take you to be my wife in faithfulness, and you will know the LORD" (2:19–20).

- "I will have compassion on Lo-ruhamah; I will say to Lo-ammi: You are my people, and he will say, 'You are my God' " (2:23).

- "I will heal their apostasy; I will freely love them, for my anger will have turned from him. I will be like the dew to Israel; he will blossom like the lily and take root like the cedars of Lebanon. ... The people will return and live beneath his shade" (14:4–5, 7).

The story that Hosea tells is a love story, but not the kind anyone would expect. It's a love story between a faithful, compassionate God and his ever-wandering people. Can you see how the very sorts of people who obviously don't make the grade are the ones God loves to love? Hosea, Gomer, and her children had one reputation. But God gave them another. He called them his own. They only needed to believe he was that good. So do we. We need to transfer our trust away from our ability to earn love and on to Jesus, the one who lived perfectly, died shamefully, and rose triumphantly so that he could give us a new name: Beloved. We can get off the meritocracy merry-go-round. We can rest in the truth that we are not good or worthy on our own. Jesus has done it all, and when he cried, "It is finished" (John 19:30), it was.

An Exemplary Family and Two Apostles

It would be reasonable to think that the living parable of Hosea and Gomer's marriage was only for people in Old Testament times. But, never one to waste anything, the Spirit inspired both

Paul and Peter to employ this story for New Testament believers. Paul wanted to show them (and us) that God's welcome wasn't based on our ancestry or choice but rather because of his unmerited grace. He writes,

> And what if he did this [freely showed mercy to the undeserving] to make known the riches of his glory on objects of mercy that he prepared beforehand for glory—on us, the ones he also called, not only from the Jews but also from the Gentiles? As it also says in Hosea,
>
>> I will call Not My People, My People,
>> and she who is Unloved, Beloved.
>> And it will be in the place where they were told,
>> you are not my people,
>> there they will be called the sons of the living God.
>> (Romans 9:23–26)
>
> What should we say then? Gentiles, who did not pursue righteousness, have obtained righteousness—namely the righteousness that comes from faith. (Romans 9:30)

Paul was thinking about Gomer, our representative sinner, when he wrote, "I will call *Not My People, My People*, and she who is *Unloved, Beloved*" (Romans 9:25).

Look at that again. We are just like Gomer. We are frail and unbelieving, but we are his. We are beloved. We don't need to build our own reputation, legacy, or proof of great faith, to know we're okay, to know we're saved. We are already loved. We have nothing left to prove.

Peter, too, was thinking of Gomer when he wrote about us, the church, in this way: "Once you were not a people, but now you are God's people; you had not received mercy, but now you have received mercy" (1 Peter 2:10).

This is what I know about you: you long to know that you are worthy of love. You try to accomplish this by looking at your life and counting up the good things you've done. You want to rest in your own righteousness, to know that you're worthy of being loved. I get that. The desire to think you are making the grade resides in all our hearts. It's the place where our fight to believe will be the hardest. Like you, I have to fight to believe in his love every day, especially on the days when I can't boast in my own goodness and feel like a complete failure. But the fight is also there when I think I'm nailing it and then wonder at the trials that pop up in my life. I swing back and forth between feeling like a loser who doesn't deserve anything to being frustrated because I don't feel like I deserve the suffering I'm facing. I must fight to believe that I am beloved because God has chosen to call me that. It's always a fight for me, but I'm in good company. It was also a fight for the apostle Paul:

> For we are the ... ones who worship by the Spirit of God, boast in Christ Jesus, and do not put confidence in the flesh. ... But everything that was a gain to me, I have considered to be a loss because of Christ. More than that, I also consider everything to be a loss in view of the surpassing value of knowing Christ Jesus my Lord. Because of him I have suffered the loss of all things and consider

them as dung, so that I may gain Christ and be found in him, not having a righteousness of my own from the law, but one that is through faith in Christ—the righteousness from God based on faith. My goal is to know him and the power of his resurrection and the fellowship of his sufferings, being conformed to his death, *assuming that I will somehow reach* the resurrection from among the dead.

Not that I have already reached the goal or am already perfect, but *I make every effort to take hold of it* because I also have been taken hold of by Christ Jesus. (Philippians 3:3, 7–12)

Do you hear the struggle in Paul's heart? He built his whole life on personal obedience to God's law, to righteousness in a meritocracy, but now we see him counting everything he had relied on before as dung. His one desire is to know Christ and live in the light of all that Jesus has done. That is his daily struggle.

Refusal to put confidence in ourselves is not an easy thing to do, especially when we have been told over and over again that God gives goodies to people who are good; that we are workers in a meritocracy. We have to fight the lie that whispers to us, *Just try harder. ... Just be better. ... You can earn God's blessings in your life*. And we must fight it at every turn.

We also have to fight against the voice that whispers lies about what a blessed, beloved life looks like. Those pictures we see on social media of perfect children smiling sweetly and beautifully crafted coffee drinks are marketing tools of a meritocracy. It's sad to say, but in them we've constructed dream palaces in our imagination and have assumed that if we really were loved and blessed by God, our lives would look a certain way. But even so, no matter what our lives look like, whether good or bad, we should never judge God's love for us by this standard. Our fight is to believe that we are beloved, even when, to our eyes, the opposite seems true. My suffering is real, but God's promise of love is everlasting.

Seeing the Good News in a Shocking Story

I want to believe that once Gomer experienced the love of a godly man and had a family, she turned from her wickedness. But she didn't. She left Hosea and went back to her life of debauchery. Shockingly, God told Hosea to go out and buy her back from her new master. Think of that. Perhaps Hosea thought that God would change her, free him from her, or that his obedience would ultimately earn him a blessed life. But the Lord had another plan. It was a plan to send his righteous and holy son to marry a wicked, debauched woman to prove what love really looked like and to free this broken woman from all her efforts to save herself.

The church is this woman. The church is modern-day Gomer. She fought to prove she was free and had agency to do as she pleased. She thought she needed to provide for herself (Hosea 2:5). What she needed to understand was that she was truly loved and all she needed had already been given to her. Whether she ever understood that is not something we're told. Hosea preached the gospel in his day. In speaking for God he said, "I will take you to be my wife forever. I will take you to be my wife in righteousness, justice, love, and compassion.

I will take you to be my wife in faithfulness, and you will know the Lord" (2:19–20). What words of comfort poor, bereft Hosea, preached to sinners! Did anyone listen? We don't know. He was like the Lord Jesus, who spread out his hands in love to a wayward people, "How often I wanted to gather your children together, as a hen gathers her chicks under her wings, but you were not willing!" (Matthew 23:37). By his life spent in service to an adulterous wife and an adulterous nation, Hosea preached God's loving grace to sinners. But they "were not willing."

If we live our lives trying to prove we're worthy of love by our successes, seeking merit by our achievements, we will be disappointed. That's because God's ways are not our ways. He defines success as a life lived in faith, in believing that he loves the unsuccessful. He gives us his righteousness. The loving work of the Lord Jesus speaks this beautiful truth to us, people who do not deserve to hear it. We need to remember that, as Duane A. Garrett notes in his commentary, it is God's perfect "compassion by which he saves and communicates his righteousness to his people. *God pays the coin of grace to obtain the bride he loves.*"[1]

Here are words from another prophet, Isaiah, about you, your belovedness, and your new name:

> You will no longer be called Deserted,
> and your land will not be called Desolate;
> instead, you will be called My Delight Is in Her,
> and your land Married;
> for the LORD delights in you,
> and your land will be married.

> For as a young man marries a young woman,
> so your sons will marry you;
> and as a groom rejoices over his bride,
> so your God will rejoice over you. (Isaiah 62:4–5)

And,

> "For the LORD has called you,
> like a wife deserted and wounded in spirit,
> a wife of one's youth when she is rejected,"
> says your God. (Isaiah 54:6)

As we close this chapter, think once again about the life of Hosea. He was a righteous, obedient man who chose the hard path that God had laid out before him. If he had wanted the approval of those around him, if he had tried to earn merit through his neighbor's opinions, he would never have walked into the hard obedience God called him to. As a living parable of God's opinion of his adulterous people, Hosea's obedience to God's command would have disqualified him from serving as a priest by marrying a woman defiled by prostitution (see Leviticus 21:7). In obeying God's call for him to "Go and marry a woman of promiscuity" (Hosea 1:2), Hosea would not only have been barred from service as a priest; he would have also placed himself outside the bounds of respectful religious society.

Despite his faithful obedience, Hosea's ministry wasn't successful. Israel's northern kingdom, his primary audience, was taken into captivity within a few decades of his prophecies. If he were trying to earn merit by turning wayward Israel back to Yahweh her husband, he would have been a failure.

But in God's eyes, he was a success because he believed. God proclaims, even today, that his work meant something. It wasn't just for himself or even the people of his time that he was working. It was for us, so that we could see what the heart of God is like. Hosea's voice still speaks to us today—not primarily as a man who was perfectly obedient but as someone who believed in the love of God for sinners, even himself. Hosea understood God's grace for the wayward. Because of that, he has been given the perfect record of Jesus Christ, the one who married a whore (the church) and continued to love her, giving her his good name, no matter how many times she failed.

Digging Deeper

1. How do Hosea's prophecy and life declare the good news?

2. How does God's love for Gomer and her children shatter meritocracy? Why is that good news for you?

3. What does it mean to try to earn merit for yourself? Are you aware of any specific ways you do this?

4. Why do you think the book of Hosea is in the Bible?

5. How does this book confront the ways we normally think about a life of faith? How does it confront your beliefs?

6. Summarize what you've learned in this chapter in four or five sentences.

3

Too Wonderful to Believe

Let's gather together for another story that wouldn't work well for flannelgraph story time, shall we? The main characters in this tale are Abraham and Sarah—famous believers who were also confused, deceitful, selfish, faithless, abusive, and unloving. If they were judged on their merit, they would be considered epic failures. But they were also recipients of a grace that transformed their failures into fulfilled promises.

Sarah is important to both the Old and New Testament church. Aside from her story in Genesis, she is also mentioned in Isaiah, Romans, and Hebrews. In fact, Peter holds her up as a woman to emulate and even calls her our spiritual mother (1 Peter 3:6). Judging from this reputation, you might assume she lived an exemplary life and earned an A in meritocracy. It would also be easy to assume that a woman so respected would certainly have had a great marriage and, if perhaps not exactly perfect, would have experienced all the blessings of living in faith. Right? Well, yes, she was blessed. But not, perhaps, in the ways we would expect.

The Backstory

Around 1900 BC, years before the birth of Jesus, Abraham and Sarah lived in Mesopotamia (likely modern-day Iraq). They lived with Abraham's grandfather, Nahor, who was the father of Terah. Terah had three sons: Abraham, Nahor (named after the family patriarch), and Haran. As it was quite common in those days for cousins and even half-siblings to marry, Nahor married Milcah, his cousin, and Abraham married Sarah, his half-sister. Sarah was the daughter of Abraham's father, Terah, but by a different mother. Marrying within one's family was beneficial for many reasons, because together they could pool wealth, share labor, and protect the family.

Abraham and Sarah's marriage would undoubtedly seem shocking to us for another reason. Abraham was ten years older than his sister-wife, Sarah, and she was probably just entering into puberty when they married, so she was perhaps fourteen or so. This sounds offensive to our modern sensibilities, but, due to the dangers of life during that time and the purpose of marriage, which was to build up the family's mutual wealth, status, and might, this was culturally acceptable.

Although it is possible that Sarah loved Abraham as her older brother and was willing to become his sister-wife (though she probably didn't have much choice in the matter), we should resist the modern impulse to turn their relationship into a romance novel. They were far more focused on survival than romance. The family meant everything to them—not just because they had affection for their relatives, but because without the security and safety of the family, they would face destitution and probable death.

When Abraham was seventy-five and Sarah was sixty-five, the Lord called Abraham, an idol worshiper, to journey farther on to the land of Canaan. Then that we are told that Sarah "was unable to conceive; she did not have a child" (Genesis 11:30). While childlessness is indeed a heartbreak many experience today, in that time it was far more so. Because the primary reason for marriage was to strengthen the family, Sarah's inability to conceive was more than a personal sadness for her and Abraham. It was tantamount to failure to fulfill her responsibilities. Sarah had one job: to furnish the family with sons who would carry on the clan's name and labor in it.

We would be wrong to assume that Sarah's failure didn't affect her marriage to Abraham. Perhaps some of what we know of Abraham's cowardice, selfishness, and callousness toward her later on can be explained (but never excused) by it. Certainly, many of her later actions make sense in light of this significant reality, too. We are initially introduced to Sarah by just one sentence: twice she's referred to as a failure (see Genesis 11:30). Only one thing would have vindicated her: producing a son. And it was the one thing she couldn't do.

The Promised Blessing

But then the Lord made a shocking promise to Abraham:

> Go from your land,
> your relatives,
> and your father's house
> to the land that I will show you.
> I will make you into a great nation,

> I will bless you,
> I will make your name great,
> and you will be a blessing.
> I will bless those who bless you,
> I will curse anyone who treats you with contempt,
> and all the peoples on earth
> will be blessed through you. (Genesis 12:1–3)

That's an outrageous promise, isn't it? Especially when you consider that the couple who received it was not only childless but also aged. It's also a restatement of one that was originally given to Adam and Eve around two thousand years earlier (Genesis 3:15): a son was coming who would bless many people and defeat God's enemies. But notice: this later promise is spoken to Abraham alone. In fact, in the original text, it's spoken solely to him— we don't hear anything about the Lord speaking directly to Sarah for many years. We don't even know whether Abraham told Sarah about it. Get the picture: God promised a seventy-five-year-old man a child. And his sixty-five-year-old sister-wife hadn't been able to conceive. Certainly, this was a bleak situation to speak a promise of life into, but it was about to get worse.

Despite all this hopelessness, Abraham obeyed God and traveled to Canaan while awaiting the fulfillment of God's promise. But then a severe famine hit. So, Abraham decided to journey down to Egypt to get food. There he realized he had another problem: his wife was as beautiful as she was barren, and that endangered him because the Egyptians commonly seized pretty women for Pharaoh's harem. So, before crossing over into Egypt, he said to Sarah, "Look, I know what a beautiful woman you are. When the Egyptians see you, they will say, 'This is his wife.' They will kill me but let you live. Please say you're my sister so it will go well for me because of you, and my life will be spared on your account' " (Genesis 12:11–13).

Abraham's Betrayal

Have you ever wondered about Abraham's betrayal? I have. How could a man who loved his wife, his sister, sell her into the harem of a foreign king? Perhaps his action reveals his attitude toward her. Sure, she was beautiful, but what did that beauty matter to him when she had failed in her responsibility to the family? His words to her are pretty much a command. In common parlance, we might translate him as saying, "Listen up!" We don't hear Sarah's response, but it's not as though she had any choice in the matter. She knew she was useless, and it really didn't matter whether God had made a promise to Abraham or not. It certainly didn't concern her. Perhaps she thought that going willingly into Pharaoh's harem was the least she could do to spare the patriarch from suffering violence on her account. So, she did. How would we illustrate *that* on our flannelgraph?

Please notice that the Bible does not say she was protected from Pharaoh's use of her. In fact, Pharaoh himself said, "I took ['seized,' 'married,' or 'acquired'] her as my wife" (Genesis 12:19). It's hard to read this story, including all the riches Pharaoh showered on Abraham for his use of Sarah (Genesis 12:16), without concluding that, in essence, Abraham pimped her out to Pharaoh. While the Lord eventually delivered her by afflicting Pharaoh's household, this didn't happen overnight. We don't know how long Sarah was in Pharaoh's harem, but it was long enough for God's judgment to be recognized by him. Again, I want you to get the picture: at this point the relationship between Abraham and Sarah was simply one of habit, convenience, and convention. She was expendable. Perhaps he was even glad to be rid of her; maybe he thought of her as the reason God's promise hadn't yet been fulfilled. She stood in the way of his receiving the promised blessing. All that ultimately mattered to Abraham was the endurance of the clan and the fulfillment of God's promise. Sarah was useless. She was unloved. Nothing aside from motherhood would vindicate her, and that wasn't something she could produce.

Despite Abraham's faithlessness, Sarah was beloved by God. He hadn't forgotten her. She was valued and cherished. So, he fought for her, and she was eventually released from Pharaoh's harem. Despite all Abraham's bad behavior, once again God renewed his covenant with him, even though he still failed to really believe the promise. Relying on his own plans to achieve God's promise, Abraham suggested that a home-born slave, Eliezer, would suffice. In response, the Lord promised, "One who comes from your own body will be your heir" (Genesis 15:4). At last, it seems that Abraham did believe, at least for a moment, because the Lord "credited it to him as righteousness" (Genesis 15:6). Abraham is justified or declared righteous not because he was able to produce offspring, or even because he was such a stellar example of a godly husband. He was declared righteous because he believed in God's promises.

Here's another picture of the good news: Abraham was a broken sinner who was counted as a righteous person because he believed in God's good promise that, through him, there would be a son born who would bless the whole world. Thank God! Abraham's righteousness came to him by faith alone, the same way ours comes to us. Abraham is judged or counted as righteous solely because he trusted God's promise. It was Abraham's belief *alone*, not his obedience or faithful actions (where were they?), that caused him to earn the reputation of righteous in God's eyes. When we think about our own salvation, we see that it, too, is all of grace.

Sarah's Scheme

At last we hear Sarah's voice, though what we hear is heartbreaking, "Since the LORD has prevented me from bearing children, go to my slave; perhaps through her I can build a family" (Genesis 16:2).

It had been ten years since the original promise of a son had been given to Abraham. Ten years. Sarah was now seventy-five years old, and her situation was even more hopeless. She had no value in her husband-brother's eyes. She was desperate. She had no way to earn respect and love. She could not justify herself in her own eyes or the eyes of the clan. That Abraham didn't love her had been made blatantly clear. So, she looked at her Egyptian slave and thought, *Maybe I can fulfill my responsibilities and be vindicated through her. I certainly paid dearly enough for her.*

I've often heard Sarah maligned for giving Hagar to Abraham. But her hopelessness didn't differ much from Abraham's. He didn't believe God would protect him. He didn't think Sarah could conceive. He thought she was worthless and couldn't see how she would be a part of God's plan, which is why he looked at his servant/slave Eliezer and thought, *This is how I will make it work.* Sarah looked at her servant/slave Hagar and assumed the same thing: that she must come up with a plan to fulfill God's impossible promise. The Lord was quick to reject Abraham's plan, but Sarah was allowed to put hers into action, at least for a season.

We will look more closely at Hagar's life later, but for now, it's important that we don't view this story through our modern lens, as if it happened today. During Abraham's time, it was very common for patriarchs, especially childless ones, to take co-wives, concubines, or even female slaves to produce heirs. So, Sarah gave Hagar to her husband in her quest for vindication, but her desires were thwarted once again. As we so often do, Sarah was still trying to earn God's love and promise, when he was offering both as a gift. She just needed to wait. But waiting is so hard, isn't it?

Hagar did indeed conceive, but when she discovered she was pregnant, she treated Sarah with contempt. For Sarah, this was just the last straw. Listen to how she spoke to Abraham: "You are responsible for my suffering! I put my slave in your arms, and when she saw that she was pregnant, I became contemptible to her. May the Lord judge between me and you" (Genesis 16:5).

Think about Sarah's words: "You are responsible for my suffering! ... May the Lord judge between me and you." Sarah was filled with wrath. In fact, she sounded like an abused woman. She blamed Abraham for her suffering. He might have gone along with her plan, but he still failed to treat her with love and respect. To make matters worse, his attitude toward her was now being mimicked by his lover, her slave.

Although her wrath might seem like an overreaction, to understand this story from Sarah's perspective, we might consider the things she had suffered and for how long. She was ashamed and humiliated. Everyone knew what Abraham thought of her. Now, an Egyptian slave, of all people, was mocking her. She had become contemptible, "slight, trifling, of little account," to Hagar.[2] For Sarah, this was the last straw. When women who have suffered abuse for years finally speak, it's frequently in very strong, almost offensive language. This doesn't excuse unkind actions; it simply makes them more understandable. Like them, Sarah had been humiliated one too many times. Her husband had humiliated her. Pharaoh humiliated her. Her barrenness had mocked her empty womb. And now this Egyptian slave had joined them. Sarah's shame and rage had been building up for decades. So, she challenged the Lord to decide between them: *Who was in the wrong?* In sin and grief, Sarah poured out on Hagar all her pent-up wrath, treating her so abusively that Hagar eventually ran away.

The God Who Sees and Blesses

Later, after Hagar returned, the child was born, and he is described as "Abraham's" son, not Sarah's (or even Hagar's), as he should have been. Abraham accepted Ishmael as the child of promise, and the door of hope was slammed shut in Sarah's face. She continued to view herself as useless baggage, and Abraham thought he could fulfill God's promise without her.

Thirteen years later, God again appeared to Abram and changed his name to Abraham, declaring that he had already made him the "father of many nations" (Genesis 17:5). But now, for the first time, Sarah was included, too. "I will bless her," God declared (17:16). The Lord changed Sarai's name to Sarah, and he gave her a new identity, too. She would not be the same person she had been. She would be blessed of God: "I will bless her; indeed, I will give you a son by her. I will bless her, and she will produce nations; kings of peoples will come from her." (17:16). The first words we hear directly spoken by the Lord about Sarah are words of blessing: "I will bless her. … I will bless her." Notice that God pronounced blessing on her twice. Remember how Sarah had been described before? Twice her barrenness was declared. Now, twice, God promised her blessing. The childless woman would be blessed. The barren woman would be the mother of nations.

Even though she was hidden away in the tent, Sarah was seen by the Lord. "Where is your wife Sarah?" asked the Lord (Genesis 18:9). It's not as though he didn't know where she was. It was rather that he wanted her to know that her days of being invisible and unseen were over. *I see her, and I will bless her*. Sarah heard these words but couldn't believe them. Sarah laughed to herself, saying, "After I am worn out and my lord is old, will I have delight?" (18:12). In her unbelief, she spoke like an abused woman. Then God posed a question: "Is anything too hard for the LORD?" (18:14 NIV). The word that's translated "hard" here actually means "marvelous" or "wonderful." The Lord is saying that his way is better than Sarah can even imagine. He is wonderfully powerful. He is the marvelous God who can bring to life lifeless wombs. After decades of hopelessness and denigration, it is not surprising that Sarah laughed in unbelief. In fact, it would have been surprising if she hadn't. Perhaps we should remember her history and give her more grace when remembering this part of her story.

Even though God made it clear that he saw and valued Sarah, Abraham sold her into the hand of another pagan king, Abimelech. But this time, God intervened, vindicating her by declaring her worth and beloved status. He protected her when Abraham wouldn't. Once Abimelech realized she was Abraham's wife, he spoke to Sarah, "I am giving your brother one thousand pieces of silver. It is a verification of your honor to all who are with you. You are fully vindicated" (Gen 20:16). Such beautiful words, though spoken by a pagan king. Sarah was vindicated. The words she had longed to hear her entire life were not spoken to her by her husband but by a pagan king. Before she had proven her worth to her husband and family by birthing a son, before she had fulfilled any of her obligations, she was freely justified by God's gracious gift. She was told, "You are fully vindicated," freed from the disdain and disrespect of any who might question her worth.

The good news of the gospel is that those words are for us, too. No one, not even the one who accuses Christ's brothers and sisters, has any voice left. He has been thrown down

(Revelation 12:10). Remember that Christ, the one who lived our life with and for us, will never accuse us. We are vindicated by faith alone even though many times our faith is nearly nonexistent. But even if it is the size of a mustard seed, it is enough. You are vindicated. Counted righteous. Beloved. "The Lord came to Sarah as he had said, and the Lord did for Sarah what he had promised to do. Sarah became pregnant and bore a son to Abraham. ... Abraham named his son who was born to him—the one Sarah bore to him—Isaac. ... Sarah said, 'God has made me laugh, and everyone who hears will laugh with me. ... Yet I have borne a son for him in his old age'" (Genesis 21:1–3, 6–7).

Sarah was finally vindicated and Abraham was justified, too, but that doesn't mean either one of them was sinless. Just when she thought it would be impossible to laugh with joy instead of hopelessness, God surprised Sarah. In time though, Sarah's laughter turned again to rage as she exiled Hagar and her son for laughing at Isaac's weaning. Sarah's story shows us how often we are both the abused and the abuser, the rejected and the rejector. We are all such broken people. Broken but beloved.

The Joy of Vindication

We don't hear anything more about Sarah until her death. We don't know what she thought about the test of Abraham and Isaac. But there is one thing we do know. We know that at her death Abraham "mourn[s]" and "weep[s]" for her (Genesis 23:1). It's the only time we hear that Abraham mourned anything. And her grave was the only plot of land that Abraham ever owned in the Promised Land (23:19–20). Finally, after her death, we see

Sarah as beloved in the eyes of her brother-husband. But more importantly, she was beloved in the eyes of her Lord. She lived as the unloved one, but finally she was vindicated. Finally, she discovered her belovedness.

Scripture teaches us that Jesus entered into every trial and temptation that Sarah, Abraham, and we share (Hebrews 2:14). Like us, he knows what it's like to be thought of as nothing: he had no honor in his own hometown. He knows what it's like to be looked down on, as he was pejoratively called a "carpenter's" son, a son of Belial. Where is his reward for perfect obedience to the law? Although he was called beloved by his Father several times in his life, he was empty, fruitless, powerless, and alone on Calvary. This is where he and Sarah, and all of us, share the same experience: in this sin-cursed world we feel alone, exiled, and forsaken. We join him in his cry: "Why am I forsaken?" Unlike the perfect Son of God, of course, we know that our aloneness is in part because of our own sin and the sins of others against us. Abraham sold Sarah into a harem to protect himself. But Jesus was sold to a Roman cross because of our fruitlessness, our failures, and of course, ultimately for the protection of his clan, his family. His death protected the survival of his clan, his family (John 11:49–50).

Our Better Brother-Husband

Jesus is the betrayed and forsaken one. He is our righteous Brother-Husband who stepped into danger and death to protect his beautiful, beloved, and barren ones. He protects us from slavish captivity to Satan. We are all looking for a righteous

Brother-Husband. Even for those of us who have good marriages, as I do, our spouses are unable to fully live up to that perfect ideal. Jesus is the only Savior we need. Jesus is our perfect, brave, loving Brother-Husband. And he's here to stay. When Sarah said to her husband, Abraham, "You are responsible for my suffering," she was speaking the very words that Jesus could say to us. But he didn't. He absorbed all the disrespect and accusations hurled at him and was silent before his attackers. He overcame their hatred out of righteous love.

It's easy to look at the life of Sarah and miss the heartaches she suffered, or to just focus on the anger or unbelief she displayed. We need to remember that she was abandoned, betrayed, and humiliated. She had clawed her way through decades of unfulfilled dreams and deep disrespect and danger. Even so, the apostle Peter showcases her as the example of a godly, courageous woman: "For in the past, the holy women who put their hope in God also adorned themselves in this way, submitting to their own husbands, just as Sarah obeyed Abraham, calling him lord. You have become her children when you do what is good and do not fear any intimidation" (1 Peter 3:5–6).

This testimony about Abraham and Sarah's life teaches us that when God vindicates and justifies us, our vindication is complete. We can hope in God, even when it seems as though all our hopes and plans have disintegrated before our eyes. Sarah is held forth as an example of holiness and faith. Think of that and let it comfort you. No matter how you have failed or even continue to, if you have been vindicated by the perfect life, death, and resurrection of Jesus, you are called a holy man or woman by faith.

Even amid our troubles, we have no reason to doubt God's love. We can be assured that we are beloved even when we've been betrayed, as Sarah was. Jesus, our faithful Brother-Husband, is the ultimate one who was abandoned and betrayed. He did this for us so that we would rest in the assurance that we'll always be cherished. No matter our circumstances, we can know that God sees and values us.

I admit, it's easy for me to believe that right now, as I sit writing on my patio in the beautiful San Diego sunshine. But does God see me when it's 2 a.m. and I'm struggling with arthritis pain or anxiety over the future? Does he really see me as I wonder what the years ahead may hold for Phil and me as we enter our final decades? I remember all the ways I've failed the Lord. Will he ever actually vindicate me?

This is the time when I have to rest again in the vindication he's granted me. I am justified. Not because I have fulfilled all the expected obligations. Not because I have been a good wife, daughter, sister, or friend. Not because I have been fruitful in all the ways I hoped I would be. I have failed countless times and for more years than I care to number. Sarah is my sister. She is my mother. I'm just like her. I listen too closely to what others say about me. I long for their approval. I want to justify myself and earn my reward.

As we think about Sarah's story, we must remember the question the Lord asked her: "Is anything impossible [too wonderful, too marvelous] for the Lord?" (Genesis 18:14). And we can remember another time when similar words were spoken to Mary, whose pregnancy was just as impossible as Sarah's (Luke 1:37).

Try filling in the following blank with your own name: _____ is a holy woman or man of God who does what is right without being intimidated, no matter what.

Jesus, our Husband-Brother, whose birth was impossible, has made a proclamation about us: We are vindicated. We are justified. We are beloved. Rest here, my sisters and brothers. It is the only place our tired hearts—worn out from trying and failing—can find peace.

Digging Deeper

1. What did you learn in this chapter about the life of people in ancient times? How did understanding these things affect your view of Abraham and Sarah's actions?

2. Peter refers to Sarah as a woman who does what is right without being intimidated. Why do you think Peter says this about her? Where do we tend to see the opposite in her life?

3. What would doing "what is good without being afraid" mean in your life? What fears motivate you to do things you know you shouldn't do?

4. Read Hebrews 11:11–16. How is Sarah described here? How does that encourage you?

5. What would it mean to "die in faith" and yet not receive "the things that are promised"? What does it mean to you personally? Why is faithful perseverance important?

6. Summarize what you've learned in this chapter in four or five sentences.

4

Beloved Outcasts, Hagar and Photine

Since we are trying to see what the life of faith outside the boundaries of a meritocracy looks like, perhaps we should just put away the flannelgraph for a while. Very little in the world of unearned blessing lavished on unworthy sinners is flannelgraph appropriate, and the stories in this chapter are no different. God's lavish grace doesn't fit neatly into morality tales illustrated with paper dolls.

Let us consider now the lives of two unnamed women and one unexpected man who loved them. Although their stories occurred thousands of years apart, they are similar in many ways. Both women were thirsty, and both visited wells that were crucial sources of life.

Outwardly, these wells looked like nothing more than holes in the ground, but they were the places their lives would be forever changed. One woman came to the well in the heat of the day, to fulfill her demanding responsibilities. The other woman found rest by one, thinking she might die under the blazing sun. As she lay there, suffering in the fierce heat, she assumed her short and miserable life would soon be over. But she was wrong. In fact, they were both wrong, because they both assumed they were unloved.

Aside from their mutual dependence on a well, both women also shared an astonishing encounter, one that no one could have predicted. Amid the desperate ordinariness of life, revelation broke through. The Water of Life spoke to them, and they were invited to drink deeply and discover the love and calling they had been longing for. They were about to discover that they were beloved.

The First Unnamed Woman

We know the first of these two unnamed women as Hagar, Sarah's slave and ultimately the mother of Ishmael. We call her unnamed not because we don't know her name but because those who owned her never referred to her as Hagar. To them, she was always just "the slave."

As you'll recall, although God had promised Abraham descendants as innumerable as the stars in the sky (Genesis 15:5), his wife, Sarah remained childless. As time ground on, Sarah became more and more desperate to conceive. So, she decided to use her slave—her property—Hagar as a surrogate to birth a son for her. Although we don't know when Hagar became part of Abraham's clan, one possibility is that she was part of the wage earned by Sarah when Abraham bought Pharaoh's favor by selling her into his harem. In any case, Sarah owned Hagar. Hagar was also an Egyptian, which meant that she was not part of the people of the promise, although that probably didn't matter to her. She was just trying to survive and likely didn't have the time or inclination to be curious about God's promises to her master. She didn't have any blessing or future she could hold on to. She was undoubtedly an idol worshiper. She was a woman without rights, standing, or possessions, who had no hope of ever improving her situation. To her owners, she was chattel, a nameless piece of property. Her existence depended solely on pleasing her owners, so when Sarah gave her for Abraham's use, she would have had no say in the matter. The weight of failed responsibility had pressed heavily on Sarah for decades, so she used Hagar in a wicked way in an attempt to fix her situation.

Once Hagar discovered she was pregnant, she began to treat Sarah with contempt. We aren't told why her attitude changed like this; perhaps her pregnancy freed her to finally express her displeasure and fight for a name of her own. Perhaps she even looked at her relationship with Abraham as a way to earn a higher standing in the clan and make a name for herself. She may have thought she would assume Sarah's place of power. For whatever reason, Hagar's attitude toward Sarah changed, and she began to look down on Sarah. When Sarah saw this change in Hagar, she complained to Abraham, blaming him for the way Hagar treated her. Once again, Abraham demonstrated his lack of care for the women in his life by responding, "Your slave is in your power; do whatever you want with her" (Genesis 16:6). Not only did Abraham not care about this woman he had impregnated, but neither did he care about the child growing within her or the abuse she suffered. He didn't even call her by name. She was simply Sarah's "slave."

In any case, Abraham's response soon garnered an even stronger one from Sarah, her owner. Sarah had too many years of being treated with contempt, especially after Abraham had given her to Pharaoh. To be treated in this way now, by someone she considered worthless Egyptian "trash," was more than she could bear. The abused became the abuser, and Hagar ran for her life. She was a poor, nameless, exiled, unwed pregnant girl, without anyone to protect her, not even the father of the child growing within her. Perhaps she decided to run away in the hope that she might make it back to Egypt. But instead of finding her way back to her earthly homeland, her journey led her to a "spring in the wilderness," where this lost woman was found and finally found a home in God.

Seeking and Saving the Lost

Here's the narrative from Genesis 16:6–11:

> Then Sarai mistreated her so much that she ran away from her.
>
> The angel of the LORD found her by a spring in the wilderness. ... He said, "Hagar, slave of Sarai, where have you come from and where are you going?"
>
> She replied, "I'm running away from my mistress Sarai."
>
> The angel of the LORD said to her, "Go back to your mistress and submit to her authority." The angel of the LORD said to her, "I will greatly multiply your offspring, and they will be too many to count."

> The angel of the LORD said to her, "You have conceived and will have a son. You will name him Ishmael, for the LORD has heard your cry of affliction."

In her exhaustion, she stopped by a well to quench her thirst. It was there that her story took a turn neither she nor anyone could have anticipated. We learn that pre-incarnate Christ, in the form of the "angel of the LORD," was searching for her. And he "*found* her by a spring in the wilderness." The Hebrew here indicates that the Lord found her after seeking or searching for her. Out in the middle of nowhere, the Second Person of the Trinity, the Son, came, searching for this lost woman, looking for the one he loved. Think of that. Hagar hadn't been seeking God. It probably never occurred to her that there was a God aside from Ra. But, unlike Ra, this God was personal. Here we see Hagar named for the first time: "Hagar, slave of Sarai" (Genesis 16:8). The speaker knew her name and why she was running. Sure, he knew the name of her powerful owner, but he also knew the name of the insignificant slave, even the name of the child who grew within her.

In a meritocracy, we hear that God blesses only those who seek him first. But Hagar's story tells us something different. Hagar wasn't seeking God. She wasn't seeking holiness, righteousness, or even grace. She was simply seeking a drink of water and a place where she wouldn't be abused while she struggled through her pregnancy. But she heard her name.

As she sat down by the well, the name-speaker broke into her isolation and exile. No, she wouldn't return to Egypt, at least not yet. She was about to be invited into her true home in Yahweh, the father of the fatherless (Psalm 68:5). Hagar's life reminds us that the Lord sees and loves the downtrodden:

> [The Lord] executes justice for the fatherless and the widow, and loves the resident alien, giving him food and clothing. (Deuteronomy 10:18)

> The LORD protects resident aliens
> and helps the fatherless and the widow. (Psalm 146:9)

A meritocracy deceives us by insisting that we can judge the strength of God's love for us by the amount of money we have in the bank, how our children are succeeding, or how our plans for the future are coming together. In fact, the opposite is true. Those who look most unloved are frequently his dearly beloved. This perspective is one of the reasons we should never assume that God's blessing in our lives will look like sweet Instagram reels filled with cute puppies and perfectly curated morning routines. Rather, we should not be surprised to see the Lord's blessing and grace lavished on both the homeless encampment and within a faithful home where there are no obvious needs. The Lord is with the fatherless and the widow, the unprotected and unprovided for, the struggling, and the one without a good name or any name at all. He seeks and finds those who know they are sick and need a physician.

The Unnamed Namer

Despite all these truths, what comes next is so absolutely

shocking that, if it weren't plainly written in Scripture, we would never believe it. "So she named the LORD who spoke to her: 'You are El-roi,' for she said, 'In this place, have I actually seen the one who sees me?'" (Genesis 16:13). Hagar, the slave without a name, *named God*. Yes, you read that right. Hagar, the unnamed, unwed Egyptian slave girl, was the *first* namer of God. Before Abraham called God El Shaddai (Genesis 17), his pregnant concubine had already named him El Roi. The Lord's condescension in seeking her out and then receiving from her lips the name El Roi should astonish us all.

El Roi means "the living One who sees me." Why that name? Hagar was undoubtedly familiar with Ra, the sun god of Egypt. But he was dead and certainly wouldn't be bothered seeing, or speaking to a worthless slave woman. But here, Hagar learns that the Lord both hears (16:11) and sees (16:13) her sorrow. How gloriously shocking!

Hagar was not a natural-born part of God's covenant people. What was Hagar's destiny and legacy? She was just part of the list of Abraham's possessions, along with the livestock "and female slaves" (Genesis 12:16). Listed there, among the flocks, herds, camels, and donkeys, Hagar's past and bleak future were written and permanently fixed. Or so she must have thought. But like Hannah after her, Hagar joined the sisterhood of all oppressed women who have not only known life on the trash heap but also have learned of the Lord's surprising intervention and condescension. "He raises the poor from the dust and lifts the needy from the trash heap. He seats them with noblemen and gives them a throne of honor" (1 Samuel 2:8).

The angel of the Lord raised Hagar up from the dust. She was lifted from the trash heap, where her owner and her own powerlessness had left her. But she would now be seated with "noblemen" on a "throne of honor." Think of that. She would have been shocked to know that, four thousand years after she met the God who saw and heard her cries, modern readers like us would rejoice in what her life and legacy show us.

What did this meeting with the Lord mean to Hagar, the woman who had never been heard or seen, the woman without a voice, name, or future? Frequently, the Lord comes to us in the place of our deepest wounds. The Lord didn't approach Hagar to assure her of her own righteousness. He didn't assure her of her own power in her weakness. Instead, he assured her that she was known. She was heard and seen by the most important person in the universe, and her story mattered—not only then but in the age to come.

After receiving from her lips the name El Roi, the Lord gave her a command and a surprising promise. He told her to go back and submit herself to the authority of the abusive Sarai. She would need a place to live and the protection of the clan to raise her son. And he gave her a promise: "I will greatly multiply your offspring, and they will be too many to count. ... You have conceived and will have a son" (Genesis 16:10–11). The Lord assured her that she would never be alone. She would be remembered. She had a name. Once again, the Lord promised that multitudes of people would come from Abraham, and although Hagar's offspring would not be the son of the promise, he would have many descendants. Hagar, the unwed mother, would have millions of progeny and would be forever known by name.

Hagar's life teaches us that wicked overlords cannot thwart God's love for us or his perfect purpose for our lives. Even so, I want to be clear that this doesn't mean that we should stay in situations of abuse. God had a particular plan for Hagar and Ishmael, and though we learn from it, their story is not prescriptive; it only describes what happened. Hagar's story, though powerful, doesn't tell us what we should do in our particular time and circumstance. Hagar didn't have any other options. She needed the provision and protection of Abraham's clan, so she had to return there when she was pregnant. Women who are in abusive situations should always seek to find protection and provision and to flee danger.

The Story on Replay

Hagar obeyed, returned, and gave birth to Ishmael. She and her son lived under the protection of the clan for fourteen more years, until the weaning ceremony of Isaac, Sarah's promised son. At this point, Ishmael foolishly mocked Isaac. And, once again, Sarah complained to Abraham about Hagar and demanded that he remove mother and son from his protection. Sarah insisted:

> "Drive out this slave with her son, for the son of this [still unnamed!] slave will not be a coheir with my son Isaac!"
>
> This was very distressing to Abraham because of his son. But God said to Abraham, "Do not be distressed about the boy and your slave. Whatever Sarah says to you, listen to her, because … I will also make a nation of the slave's son because he is your offspring." (Genesis 21:10–13)

The Lord made a promise to the illegitimate Ishmael. Hagar's name would be known, and her son would be as well.

True to form, Abraham didn't care about Hagar, the woman who had given birth to his son. His concern was for Ishmael alone, the one he supposed would fulfill the promise. Although he didn't want to see Ishmael go, he listened to God's command through Sarah. And again, we recognize El Roi, the God who saw and heard Hagar and her son, and who heard Sarah's voice as well.

> Abraham ... took bread and a waterskin, put them on Hagar's shoulders, and sent her and the boy away. She left and wandered in the Wilderness of Beer-Sheba. When the water in the skin was gone, she left the boy under one of the bushes and went and sat at a distance, about a bowshot away, for she said, "I can't bear to watch the boy die!" While she sat at a distance, she wept loudly.
>
> God heard the boy crying, and the angel of God called to Hagar from heaven and said to her, "What's wrong, Hagar? Don't be afraid, for God has heard the boy crying from the place where he is. Get up, help the boy up, and grasp his hand, for I will make him a great nation." Then God opened her eyes, and she saw a well. So, she went and filled the waterskin and gave the boy a drink. God was with the boy. ... And his mother got a wife for him from the land of Egypt. (Genesis 21:14–21)

Fourteen years after Hagar's first encounter with the Lord by the well at Beer-Lahai-roi, Hagar once again found herself discarded, wandering, and worthless. But this time, her circumstance was even more dire. She had been exiled from the clan, and there was no returning. And she was not alone. Her child, Ishmael, was with her. She assumed that he would die in the wilderness alongside her.

What happened to Hagar's faith in the God who saw and heard her in the wilderness? Had she forgotten about El Roi, the God she named? As troubling as her unbelief might be, the truth is, we are no different. What happens to my faith in the God who sees and hears me when I face loss and trial? Sometimes I remember his promises and his character. But all too frequently, I forget. None of us, no matter how desperately we believe, have unwavering faith. Perhaps Hagar had trouble facing the reality that here she was again, back in the same situation. This time, it was with a new depth of suffering because it wasn't just her but Ishmael, her beloved son, suffering with her. She just couldn't face the reality that he would die, after all this time and after all that God had done for her. He had been given a promise by El Roi, that his future would be with his relatives (Genesis 16:12). Why would she doubt this? Because Hagar was just like the rest of us. I, too, have been given all the promises in Scripture and the gift of salvation and the Holy Spirit, and yet I doubt. For fifty years I have lived in the beautiful promises of God, and even so sometimes all I can see is darkness and despair.

What did El Roi tell Hagar to do? "Get up, help the boy up, and grasp his hand, for I will make him a great nation." *Don't just sit there and wait to die*, he spoke from heaven. God had a plan for Hagar and Ishmael. So, he opened her eyes, and she saw her salvation. The God who saw her *opened her eyes*. The seeing God gives sight to the blind. Think of that. And *God was with the boy*. Sweet grace! "The terror that drove [Hagar] into the wilderness" also "drove her into the arms of" Jesus.[3] Just like Hagar, Jesus lived without any civil rights and was completely at the mercy of his Roman overlords. But God used those wicked officials to accomplish a shocking redemption.

The Lord heard Hagar's cry, and he also heard the voice of another woman, this one from Samaria. But this unnamed woman, who met God by a well, wasn't there because she was running away from an oppressive master. She was there simply because she needed water.

Another Unnamed Woman and an Unexpected Encounter

Now we'll look at another woman who, like Hagar, had a surprising encounter with a man at a well. This woman is usually referred to as "the Samaritan woman" or "the woman at the well." In this chapter, we'll call her Photine, as she is referred to in the Eastern Orthodox Church. I'm going to use this name for her, even though it isn't specified in Scripture. Here's Photine's story from John 4:

> Jacob's well was there, and Jesus, worn out from his journey, sat down at the well. It was about noon.
>
> A woman of Samaria came to draw water.
>
> "Give me a drink," Jesus said to her, because his disciples had gone into town to buy food.

"How is it that you, a Jew, ask for a drink from me, a Samaritan woman?" she asked him. For Jews do not associate with Samaritans.

Jesus answered, "If you knew the gift of God, and who is saying to you, 'Give me a drink,' you would ask him, and he would give you living water."

"Sir," said the woman, "you don't even have a bucket, and the well is deep. So where do you get this 'living water'? You aren't greater than our father Jacob, are you? He gave us the well and drank from it himself, as did his sons and livestock."

Jesus said, "Everyone who drinks from this water will get thirsty again. But whoever drinks from the water that I will give him will never get thirsty again. In fact, the water I will give him will become a well of water springing up in him for eternal life."

"Sir," the woman said to him, "give me this water so that I won't get thirsty and come here to draw water."

"Go call your husband," he told her, "and come back here."

"I don't have a husband," she answered.

"You have correctly said, 'I don't have a husband,' " Jesus said. "For you've had five husbands, and the man you now have is not your husband. What you have said is true."

"Sir," the woman replied, "I see that you are a prophet. Our ancestors worshiped on this mountain, but you Jews say that the place to worship is in Jerusalem."

Jesus told her, "Believe me, woman, an hour is coming when you will worship the Father neither on this mountain nor in Jerusalem. You Samaritans worship what you do not know. We worship what we do know, because salvation is from the Jews. But an hour is coming, and is now here, when the true worshipers will worship the Father in Spirit and in truth. Yes, the Father wants such people to worship him. God is spirit, and those who worship him must worship in Spirit and in truth."

The woman said to him, "I know that the Messiah is coming" (who is called Christ). "When he comes, he will explain everything to us."

Jesus told her, "I, the one speaking to you, am he." ...

Then the woman left her water jar, went into town, and told the people, "Come, see a man who told me everything I ever did. Could this be the Messiah?" They left the town and made their way to him. ...

Now many Samaritans from that town believed in him because of what the woman said when she testified, "He told me everything I ever did." (John 4:6–26, 28–29, 39)

Much has been written about Photine, and much of it denigrates her, casting her as an immoral woman. I confess, I have been guilty of this. But to cast her in this light is to miss her cultural context and what her story is meant to tell us. Of course, if she's cast as an immoral woman, then her story would tell us about the grace of God that comes to sinners. And while that's true, I don't think her failures are the primary lesson for us to learn.

First of all, even though she had been married numerous times, we shouldn't assume that every one of her marriages ended in divorce. Although having that many husbands would have been unusual, it's quite possible that many of them had died. Women married very young, when they first began to menstruate (and sometimes they were betrothed even before that), and they frequently married men who were much older and had already established their career and income. It wouldn't have been unusual for a woman to be a very young widow, and if her deceased husband didn't leave her with wealth or if she couldn't return to her father's home, she would have had to remarry. In addition, in Judaism women could not initiate divorce. So, rather than assuming she was immoral, perhaps we should assume that she had been widowed and also cast away through divorce. Aside from her five marriages, we also learn that she was currently living with a man who was not her husband. Although it's difficult, we must refrain from reading this story with twenty-first-century Western eyes. Because living alone was a practical impossibility for a woman in that time, it was quite common for men and women to live together in mutually beneficial arrangements.

If we understand marriage as a business arrangement rather than a romantic endeavor, then the woman's five marriages become significantly less scandalous. If we remember that cohabitation was a culturally acceptable alternative to contracted marriage, then her current situation becomes a practical solution rather than an indication of sexual sin. *In all of this—marriage, death, divorce, remarriage, informal marriage—the woman was not (necessarily) at fault in any way.* Her marital history was simply the consequence of her time and place.

Don't assume that she was an immoral woman and miss the true point of the story. Jesus doesn't tell her to repent. Instead, he engages her in conversation that's meant to communicate two things: that he knows her history and, like Hagar's El Roi, he sees her. Photine met someone who saw her and knew her, someone who would never leave her through death or divorce. He was the husband she had been waiting for.

"Come, see a man who told me everything." Jesus is Photine's El Roi, the one who knows, sees, and hears. And he goes on to reveal to her something he'd told no other non-Jew. She didn't recognize that, like Hagar, she was blind to the Fountain of Living Water standing right in front of her. But she wasn't blind much longer. She was the first gentile to have her eyes opened to see Jesus for who he truly was: "I know that the Messiah is coming."

Photine was looking for theological information. But she was blind, and information was not what she needed most. She needed revelation. So, Jesus opened her eyes: "I, the one speaking to you, am he." She was taught something others were blind to. Like Hagar before her, El Roi enabled her to see the one standing right in front of her. She was used to defending herself by her theological arguments, clever questions, and obfuscations. Instead, Jesus opened the eyes of her heart to see the one she had been looking for her whole life. And so she returned to her city and told the people she met someone who saw and knew her deeply. Like Hagar, this unlikely woman was the first to do something theologically significant. She was the first person to proclaim the truth about the identity of the Messiah to gentiles. She named the Messiah. He was El Roi ... the *man who told her everything she ever did.* He was Jesus of Nazareth.

In the Eastern Orthodox Church, Photine (whose name means "the enlightened one") is venerated as a martyred saint.

Jesus and His Bride

Although thousands of years apart, Hagar and Photine's lives mirror each other's. Both of them found deliverance and learned the fallacy of the "pull yourself up by your efforts" mentality. They were served and drank deeply of the refreshing water of free grace. And they were never the same.

The Lord loves the oppressed. He loves the outcast, the unwed mother, and the destitute. He loves the disappointed and heartbroken woman who is just trying to make things work. He loves people who want to argue about theology and those who worship sun gods. He loves those who have fallen on hard times and those who, although wealthy, are bereft of a legacy. He loves those with children and those without. Jesus knows what it is to be on the outside. After all, he was the exiled one, executed "outside the gate" (Hebrews 13:12). He entered into our shame, desperation, and hopelessness and has given us his record of faithfulness and fruitfulness.

Drink from This Well of Living Water

To the natural eye, Jesus looked like nothing more than a common man. There was nothing about him—no halo, no aura, or glow—that would have told you he was God incarnate. "He didn't have an impressive form or majesty that we should look at him, no appearance that we should desire him" (Isaiah 53:2). Neither did the wells where these two sisters met the God of glory look like anything more than holes in the ground. But these places were holy ground where people, just like us, were met by the glorious, searching God. And what did they learn about him? What do *we* learn about him? We learn that God seeks the lost, people who may not even be looking for him, people who are just muddling through the daily grind or, maybe, even facing the end of their lives.

These stories teach us that we are not unseen. We are not unheard. He is El Roi, the one who has seen every part of our lives. He is the one who has heard us, our protestations of faith, our hopelessness, our anger, and our despair. His eyes are open to us; his ears hear every word, every breath.

Not only does he personally see and hear us, but God has a specific plan for us. He has a vocation for us to fulfill. Perhaps it is rearing children, being a light in a dark place, or sharing with others how he knows and sees you. Don't think that, just because of your age or physical strength, your time to be used by God is past. You may not feel up to the task, but remember who he is. He is the one who said: "If anyone is thirsty, let him come to me and drink. The one who believes in me, as the Scripture has said, will have streams of living water flow from deep within him" (John 7:37–38).

You can trust him. Ask him to open your eyes to his presence in your life. Ask him to fill you with his Spirit. Ask him to help you hear his voice. It will be the Holy Spirit who gives you new life to proceed in the journey. If you believe in the source—Jesus—you will become a well of living water to those around you, even to your own heart. Your story isn't over yet. There is still plenty of water to drink, and the one serving it calls you his beloved.

Digging Deeper

1. If you had an opportunity to name God, what would you call him?

2. What is the most surprising aspect of Hagar's story to you and why?

3. What is the most surprising aspect of Photine's story to you and why?

4. How has this perspective on Hagar and Photine's life encouraged you?

5. What places in your life look like muddy holes in the ground that may actually be flowing with untapped, life-giving water?

6. Summarize what you have learned in this chapter in four or five sentences.

5

Tamar and Judah

Ready for a pop quiz? What *one* woman in the Old Testament is called righteous? Whom do you suppose would qualify for that title? Think about how you might answer while I remind you of another one of those not-so-flannelgraph-appropriate stories from the Old Testament.

Abraham and Sarah's only child, Isaac, had a son, Jacob, who fathered twelve sons through two co-wives and two of the wives' slaves. One of Jacob's two wives, Leah, was unloved, while the other, her younger sister, Rachel, was beloved by Jacob. Why? Was it because Rachel was a woman of faithful and godly character? No, she certainly wasn't (see Genesis 31). She was beloved by Jacob because she was pretty. So much for the patriarchs choosing women because of their virtue. But Leah, the unattractive, unloved wife, who had been foisted on Jacob through deception, was seen and beloved by the Lord. Even though she was the apparently unloved, consolation-prize wife, her actual status was far greater. "When the Lord saw that Leah was neglected, he opened her womb" (Genesis 29:31). The Lord knew her sorrow, so he enabled her to eventually give birth to four sons, the last of whom was named Judah. Don't miss the truth that God saw Leah's heartache and gave her sons as a sign of his love and care for her. The Lord is always showing up to care for the weak and discarded. Those whom the world denigrates, the Lord exalts. Unloved women with no outward beauty, who would hide their face in shame, are the ones the Lord loves to call "my beautiful bride."

Leah's son Judah grew up knowing that his mother was unloved by his father, Jacob. And therefore so was he. In addition, Rachel's favored son, Joseph, was a constant source of irritation and pain in his brothers' lives. Making matters worse, Joseph predicted that the family would one day bow down to him, and for his brothers this was the last straw. Collectively, they were filled with jealousy and hatred for their little brother, and he soon felt their wrath. When their opportunity finally came, they threw him into a pit, waiting for the right time to kill him, but the chance to make money presented itself first, and so they sold their little brother Joseph into slavery instead. Then, to deceive their father, Jacob, they killed a goat, drenched Joseph's special cloak in its blood, and sent it to their father as a sign of his son's death. Jacob's heart was broken: his beloved son was gone. The brothers thought that, with Joseph gone, their troubles would be too. Instead, their troubles were just beginning. Jacob's favoritism bore bitter fruit in the lives of all his children, including Joseph's elder brother Judah.

Soon Judah moved away from the clan and married a Canaanite woman, Shua, with whom he had three sons. At this point, Judah was an unloved, guilt-ridden, hard-hearted man, running from his sin and from God, trying to pretend he was someone else.

When Judah's eldest son, Er, grew up, he was given a wife named Tamar. The narrative doesn't tell us anything about their relationship, so we don't know whether Er even wanted a wife or whether he had any relationship with Tamar at all. Perhaps their marriage was just one of convention. All we know is that he displeased the Lord. For whatever reason, God "put him to death" (Genesis 38:7), leaving Tamar a childless widow in Judah's household. Though the narrator does not specify the nature of Er's evil, this word also describes the doomed men of Sodom (see Genesis 13:13). Because Tamar hadn't conceived any children with Er, Judah told his second son, Onan, to marry her and have sex with her in order to raise up children in his brother's name. Rightly judging that he would have a larger inheritance if Er didn't have any children through him, Onan used Tamar sexually but "released his semen on the ground so that he would not produce offspring for his brother" (Genesis 38:9). In this way, he used Tamar for sexual gratification, pretending to be honorable while refusing to give to her what she needed for respectability and provision: pregnancy.

Because of his selfishness and hatred of his brother, God killed Onan, too. Bereft of his two sons, Judah then promised to give his final remaining son, Shelah, to Tamar, telling her that she should wait until he was of age, living back in her father's house until then. But, like his father, Jacob (see Genesis 27; 29; 31), he deceived her in saying that she would eventually marry his youngest son. In sending her back to her father's house without the possibility of another marriage, he was consigning her to poverty and perpetual widowhood. She wouldn't be able to marry anyone else and would spend the rest of her life alone and disgraced.

In the meantime, Judah's wife, Shua, died. Judah was a broken, bereft man. He had lost two of his three sons and his wife. He had left his brothers, his father, and his homeland. Judah faced crushing losses, but he wasn't just a victim of circumstances. He had consigned his younger brother Joseph to slavery. He had broken his foolish father's heart. And his jealousy and hatred had undoubtedly shaped the way he parented his own sons.

Tamar's Risky Plan

Once Tamar discerned that she would not be given to Judah's youngest son, Shelah, she devised a plan to find vindication and raise up children in her husband Er's name. Knowing the kind of man Judah was, she waited until she heard that he had gone away to shear sheep, and then she dressed herself as a prostitute. When he saw her, he immediately propositioned her. That's all it took. He "saw her" and propositioned her. He said that he would send her a young goat in payment, but a goat was not what she was after. She knew she would need to defend herself if she had conceived. She obtained from him the two things she knew she'd need for vindication: his genetic material and his ID (Genesis 38:18).

Afterward, she returned to her home, changed back into her mourning clothes, and waited. Eventually, she found that her plan had worked. Soon Judah was told that Tamar was pregnant, but he was not told by whom. Unloving and hard-hearted as he was, he was undoubtedly happy to have a reason not to give his youngest son to her. Judah condemned Tamar and her unborn babies (for she was pregnant with twins) to death by fire. Wicked, cruel, hypocritical man. The more he sinned, the harder his heart became, and the more self-deceived he was. He was a man without pity, living in a phony edifice of his own supposed respectability. But because the Lord loved him, he was about to break in and break his heart. Judah was about to have a visit from El Roi. "As [Tamar] was being brought out [to execution], she sent her father-in-law this message: 'I am pregnant by the man to whom these items belong. ... Examine them. Whose signet ring, cord, and staff are these?'" (Genesis 38:25).

Her question, "Whose are these?" was a sledgehammer wielded by the hand of the Lord, who loved them both. Judah's hard heart was stricken. He finally saw himself for who he really was. And he knew he had been seen by the Lord.

When we read the common translation of Judah's response, "She is more in the right than I" (Genesis 38:26), it's hard not to laugh. In what sense had he been in the right at all? He had sold his little brother into slavery and lied about it to his father. He had moved away from his family and married a woman outside the covenant. He refused to give Tamar his son Shelah to raise up children for his son's name. Hebrew scholar Bruce Waltke contends that Judah's confession is better translated, "She is righteous, not I."[4] Here, at last, we have the answer to our pop quiz: Tamar (yes, that Tamar!) is the only woman called righteous in the Old Testament. Old Testament scholar David D. Pettus writes, "Judah even pronounces her 'righteous,' making Tamar the only female to receive that title in the Old Testament."[5]

Amazing! Tamar, the dear *unloved, beloved* abused woman was an instrument in the hand of God. "The continuation of the line of Judah does not come about by the righteous actions of the patriarch, but instead by the actions of 'righteous' Tamar." Tamar the righteous, Tamar the unloved, beloved! Think of that. At last Judah sees himself and his folly. And he knows that he too is loved.

This story is tricky, but we must remember not to judge Tamar by modern Christian ethics. Tamar was morally justified to act as she did. "Her actions, while dangerous for her, were within her rights. While her method was desperate, she only did what the law would have entitled her." And "in contrast to ... Judah's sinful motives, Tamar's motive is honorable."[6]

Both Tamar and Judah longed to be loved by those they loved. Judah was the fourth son of the unattractive, unloved Leah. Tamar was the twice-widowed, childless pariah. Judah longed for his father's love. Tamar longed for a child and a home.

Into this brokenness, the Lord brought a gift of grace to both Judah and Tamar in the form of two sons, a double blessing: Perez and Zerah. This son, Perez, whom Judah originally threatened to have killed in the womb, was the progenitor of the great king, David, and ultimately of Jesus Christ (see Matthew 1 and Luke 3). What does this tortuous story tell us? Waltke shows us, "Even the worst sort of sinners can enter heaven by God's redemptive grace."⁷ God used the terrible sin of Judah to accomplish his plan of blessing. Judah looked at his losses as a curse. Rather, Tamar and her children were the ultimate blessing he longed for. He found love again through these two sons.

Sometimes God blesses us by sending trials and difficulties that we don't want. Sometimes we fail to see that, even in the midst of great hardship, he has promised to bring eternal blessing through them to all those he loves. This is "another example," Nahum Sarna says, "of the biblical motif of God using human frailty for His own purposes."⁸

Judah's Repentance

God created within Judah the same heart that David prayed for in Psalm 51:10: "God, create a clean heart for me and renew a steadfast spirit within me." Judah was given a clean heart and a steadfast spirit. He would soon be able to face his loveless father, unloved mother, and jealous brothers. And he would do so as a broken widower, with three sons and a faithful daughter-in-law. It was time for him to return home. Judah experienced what Ezekiel would eventually prophesy: "I will give them integrity of heart and put a new spirit within them; I will remove their heart of stone from their bodies and give them a heart of flesh, so that they will follow my statutes, keep my ordinances, and practice them. They will be my people, and I will be their God" (Ezekiel 11:19–20; see also 36:26 and Jeremiah 32:39).

Judah's stony heart finally began to beat again. As far as Tamar's narrative is concerned, we don't hear much more about her. Evidently she lived out her life as a widow and the mother of Perez and Zerah in Judah's household. But that wasn't the end of her story. The same widow who was considered a pariah by her father-in-law, was sexually abused, and acted courageously and wisely is named in the blessing that the women speak over Ruth, another widowed outsider: "May your house become like the house of Perez, the son Tamar bore to Judah" (Ruth 4:12). Tamar's life and reputation became a blessing to future generations. The unloved became the beloved benediction; righteous Tamar, the proverbial blessing.

Noting that Tamar is the only woman called righteous in the Old Testament is not to say that she was the only righteous person, but she is the only one to whom the Holy Spirit gave that specific honor. Can you see, once again, how the Lord loves to honor those who have no honor in the eyes of the world?

Now that Judah had finally begun to embrace a correct self-appraisal, after having been brought to repentance for his sin by Tamar's piercing question, he longed for his home again. Finally he was strong enough to return to face his loveless father in humility. So Judah moved his family back to rejoin the clan. From there, he stepped forward as a chief negotiator in dealing with Pharaoh's representative, Joseph, who had become a ruler and arbiter of Egypt's wealth.

In dealing with his brothers as they negotiated for food, Joseph devised a plan to test whether they were truly repentant for the way they had treated him. He insisted that they bring his younger brother, Benjamin, back with them before he would give them any food. Of course, Jacob was loath to allow Rachel's only remaining son to leave him. Here that we see that Judah was finally willing to take on the role of protector, of the elder brother. He assured aged Jacob that he would be responsible for caring for Benjamin. He was willing to carry the burden for his little brother's safety. In Judah's anguished vow to his father, he promised: "I will be responsible for him. You can hold me personally accountable! If I do not bring him back to you and set him before you, I will be guilty before you forever" (Genesis 43:9; see also 44:32). And at last, we see a restored Judah, a mature man who had walked through great sin and loss, who was willing to love his brother and lay down his life for him. Judah became the man he was destined to be and shared the qualities of the one who stood in the gap for us all.

The Lion of the Tribe of Judah

Let's fast-forward now from the first book of the Bible to the last. In Revelation 5:5, the apostle John "wept and wept" because no one was worthy to unseal the scroll and reveal God's perfect plan of judgment and redemption to the assembled hosts of heaven. It appeared that no one had the authority to step into this conquering role of revelation. But then, we hear of a Lion who was "worthy to take the scroll and to open its seals" because he had been "slaughtered" and "purchased people for God" by his "blood from every tribe and language and people and nation." These multiethnic people were "made ... a kingdom and priests to our God and they will reign on the earth" (Revelation 5:9–10).

This Lion, of course, is the risen Lord Jesus, who willingly received his Father's disdain, took on himself every drop of righteous wrath for our wickedness, paid the cost for our release from the fires of eternal judgment, and folded us into his family that we might share in his inheritance. This one is the only one worthy enough to reveal God's plan.

But notice: Jesus is called "the Lion from the tribe of Judah" (Revelation 5:5). Now that you've seen all that Judah did, his deception and treachery, his hypocrisy and hatred, his cruelty and hard-heartedness, does that seem right to you? It seems to me that Jesus should be called the "Lion from the tribe of Joseph." After all, Joseph is the one with the good reputation who suffered at the hands of those who wanted to strip him of all honor. Joseph is the one who should be named as having heavenly authority. After all, he righteously managed his authority in Egypt and rescued his family from destitution. But ... he's not. Why does Judah, rather than Joseph, get this accolade?

Judah is counted worthy because God's kingdom is not a meritocracy, at least not in the ways we are tempted to think. Judah's honorable reputation should show us that someone else had to earn an honorable reputation for him and for us. Near the end of his story, Judah did grow into a respectable son and father, but his eventual goodness couldn't atone for what he had done in the past. But despite his shameful past, he was counted honorable because of the work of Jesus Christ. Jesus loved his earthly father, his Heavenly Father, and all his siblings perfectly. He did this for Judah and for us so that we would share in his honor. In our place, he died shamefully to protect us all from the fires of judgment like those that Judah wanted to consign Tamar to. Judah was granted grace and is freed from a meritocracy. In addition, the outsider, Tamar, is called a righteous woman, and her name is employed as a blessing among the women of Israel. Tamar, the resolute daughter of the King, refused to live out her life in ignominy, isolation, and barrenness, and instead willingly embraced danger, shame, and censure for the sake of her spouse's name. In doing so, she has become a blessing to despised and unloved women everywhere. "May you be like Tamar" is not a curse but a blessing.

Yet, there is still more for us to understand, and it has to do with Judah's final reconciliation with his father.

Jacob's Final Blessing

At the end of his life, Judah's father, Jacob, was brought to Egypt, and he called all of his sons to his bedside. In the blessings he bestowed on his sons, Jacob spoke of the future and gave voice to his thoughts about each of his sons. At last, we see Jacob's blessing on Judah, as father and son were finally reconciled. Can you imagine how these words must have healed Judah's broken heart?

> Judah, your brothers will praise you.
> Your hand will be on the necks of your enemies;
> your father's sons will bow down to you.
> Judah is a young lion—
> my son, you return from the kill.
> He crouches; he lies down like a lion
> or a lioness—who dares to rouse him?
> *The scepter will not depart from Judah*
> *or the staff from between his feet*
> *until he whose right it is comes,*
> *and the obedience of the peoples belongs to him.*

> He ties his donkey to a vine,
> and the colt of his donkey to the choice vine.
> He washes his clothes in wine
> and his robes in the blood of grapes.
> His eyes are darker than wine,
> and his teeth are whiter than milk.
>
> (Genesis 49:8–12)

Jacob's words of blessing for Judah, only slightly overshadowed by his blessings to his favored son, Joseph, speak of a man with authority, power, cunning, wealth, and even attractiveness. More importantly, this blessing came to be considered messianic in nature. Although verse 10 is difficult to translate, it's clear that the "scepter" and "staff" and the "right" to rule over people who must "obey" refer ultimately to the rule of the Messiah to come. When John heard that the only one who had the right to open the scroll in heaven was a lion from the tribe of Judah, he wouldn't have been surprised. He would have known Jacob's blessing and also the epithet from Micah 5:2: "Bethlehem Ephrathah, you are small among the clans of Judah; one will come from you to be ruler over Israel for me." This prophetic word established the precedent that Israel's monarchy would come from the tribe of Judah. From David's installation until the time of the Babylonian exile, a Judahite was always on the throne. Jesus also descended from this tribe (see Matthew 1:1–17).

So, Judah's name and reputation have been exalted for thousands of years. Christians associate Judah with their beloved Messiah: Jesus was born in Bethlehem of Judah, and in eternity he's lauded as the Lion of the tribe of Judah. Jesus's eternal reign, extending into eternity future, comes from the clan of Judah. His name is now a benediction instead of a curse, just like righteous Tamar's—and just like yours and mine. No matter your past failures, schemes, shame, and cruelties, if you have transferred your trust off yourself and your ability to make it in a meritocracy, you are now called a saint, a holy one, a sister or brother of the Son of God. You are considered part of the blessed family, beloved by your Father. So, of course, here we are again, remembering Hosea and Gomer's marriage as Paul employs it:

> I will call Not my People, My People,
> and she who is Unloved, Beloved.
> And it will be in the place where they were told,
> you are not my people,
> there they will be called sons of the living God.
>
> (Romans 9:25–26)

> Once you were not a people, but now you are God's people; you had not received mercy, but now you have received mercy. (1 Peter 2:10)

Joined inseparably to Jesus, we are beloved *forever*:

> Who can separate us from the love of Christ? ... For I am persuaded that neither death nor life, nor angels nor rulers, nor things present nor things to come, nor powers, nor height nor depth, nor any other created thing will be able to separate us from the love of God that is in Christ Jesus our Lord. (Romans 8:35, 38–39)

> The Son of God ... loved me and gave himself for me.
> (Galatians 2:20)

Like Tamar, we are declared righteous through faith in Jesus:

> But to the one who does not work, but believes on him who justifies the ungodly, his faith is credited for righteousness. (Romans 4:5)

> For just as through one man's disobedience the many were made sinners, so also through the one man's obedience the many will be made righteous. (Romans 5:19)

> One believes with the heart, resulting in righteousness, and one confesses with the mouth, resulting in salvation.
> (Romans 10:10)

Like Judah, we have been given authority to reign over our enemies through Christ:

> If we endure, we will also reign with him.
> (2 Timothy 2:12)

> And they sang a new song:
>   You are worthy to take the scroll
>   and to open its seals,
>   because you were slaughtered,
>   and you purchased people
>   for God by your blood
>   from every tribe and language
>   and people and nation.

> You made them a kingdom
> and priests to our God,
> and they will reign on the earth. (Revelation 5:9–10)

Like Judah, we have been reconciled to our Father:

> For if, while we were enemies, we were reconciled to God through the death of his Son, then how much more, having been reconciled, will we be saved by his life. And not only that, but we also boast in God through our Lord Jesus Christ, through whom we have now received this reconciliation. (Romans 5:10–11)

> Everything is from God, who has reconciled us to himself through Christ and has given us the ministry of reconciliation. That is, in Christ, God was reconciling the world to himself, not counting their trespasses against them, and he has committed the message of reconciliation to us. (2 Corinthians 5:18–19)

> Once you were alienated and hostile in your minds as expressed in your evil actions. But now he has reconciled you by his physical body through his death, to present you holy, faultless, and blameless before him. (Colossians 1:21–22)

In this not-quite-flannelgraph-appropriate story, we see a beautiful portrait of the redemption the Lord brings to even the worst sinners among us. Jesus is the one whose family tree includes Judah, the man who hated his father and brother and who, without a seeming second thought, would have sentenced his pregnant daughter-in-law (and his children) to the most horrific method of death. But, by God's grace, through a courageous, bereft woman, Judah's family line continued down to the most desired Son of all, Jesus, the Messiah. I've heard people express shock that Tamar is included in Jesus's genealogy. Perhaps we should be more surprised that Judah is there. And yet he is. Jesus, the Righteous Lord who loved his brothers and died to protect his bride, didn't hide his ancestry. He knew who his forebear was, and he claimed him as the head of his family.

Beloved, righteous Tamar: she is the lesson to every woman who has ever known loss and censure and yet rose bravely to complete the mission she was given. She suffered abuse at the hands of her husbands and entered into the humiliation of sex with her father-in-law, in faith, believing that somehow she would know vindication and relief from shame. And she is called righteous. Amazing grace.

Digging Deeper

1. Summarize Judah's history. Who was he? What is he known for?

2. Summarize Tamar's history. Who was she? What is she known for?

3. What have you heard about Tamar in the past? Have you ever heard her called "righteous"? What's your opinion about that judgment of her?

4. How does the redemption of Judah and Tamar turn a meritocracy on its head?

5. What courageous act might the Lord be asking of you?

6. Summarize what you've learned in this chapter in four or five sentences.

6

Finding Refuge under His Wings

It doesn't take a lot of scrolling on social media to discover that the question of what it means to be a woman or a man continues to be a hot-button topic. Some Christians propose that women should strive to be "feminine." These are the same people who would probably also say that men should grow beards and shoot guns, while women should excel in all things domestic, such as having babies and making sandwiches. These gender-war salvos are rife with stereotypes drawn more from the Victorian era than the Bible.

But the Victorian stereotype of the weak-kneed woman who faints at the sight of blood isn't found anywhere in Scripture. In fact, the women we see portrayed in the Bible are anything but fragile and frail. Think about the courage of Sarah in Pharaoh's harem or in giving birth as an elderly woman. Consider the determination to persevere in trial that we saw in Hagar, or the strength of character it took for Tamar to withstand her wicked husband Er's sin and Onan's sexual abuse. Consider her willingness to humiliate herself when accepting Judah's advances or her courageous readiness to confront his hypocrisy. As Eric Schumacher and I point out in *Jesus and Gender: Living as Sisters and Brothers in Christ*, the portrait of women of worth in Scripture is more like the warrior Dora Milaje in the movie *Black Panther* than the fainting and frivolous Mrs. Bennet in Jane Austen's *Pride and Prejudice*.

In this chapter, once again, we are going to consider two strong women who appeared unloved and one powerful man with a dubious heritage who stepped up to love, protect, and provide refuge for them. Only one of our characters' lives begin in a stereotypical way. But soon, even her expectations were shattered. Would she be numbered among the unloved?

The Time of the Judges

After the nation of Israel was freed from their Egyptian captivity under Moses's leadership, they wandered in the desert for forty years and eventually settled in the land of Canaan. The books of Judges and Ruth record some of what happened in the centuries before the monarchy was begun under Saul, in approximately 1052 BC.

The brief opening narrative found in the book of Ruth reveals the story of a Bethlehemite man, Elimelech, who with his wife and two sons serves as the backdrop for a tale of sorrow, persevering devotion, humiliation, backbreaking labor, and stunning reversals of fortune through God's grace.

Here's a brief sketch of the story: At a time of famine, Elimelech, his wife, Naomi, and their two sons, Mahlon and Chilion, left Bethlehem for Moab to try to find food. While in

Moab, Elimelech died, and Naomi was left a widow with her two sons. They each took Moabite women as wives, against God's command (Deuteronomy 7:3), and continued to live there in Moab for ten years. Eventually, both sons also died. Naomi was left alone, without either of her sons and without her husband. Alone, destitute, and heartbroken, Naomi's world had crashed in on her. Her husband and sons were dead, and her Moabite daughters-in-law were childless. If Naomi's life communicated anything, it was that the God her family had abandoned in Bethlehem had paid their desertion back in spades. She certainly knew that setting up a home in Moab was contrary to the Lord's commands. Did her circumstances make her assume she was unloved? Absolutely! And one might think she was, if she lived in a meritocracy.

In her destitution, however, Naomi heard, "The LORD had paid attention to his people's need by providing them food" (Ruth 1:6). What an interesting turn of phrase, isn't it? The Lord "*paid attention* to his people's need." Rather than being a god who would say, "Tough luck! You've made your bed, now sleep in it," his heart broke for his suffering, destitute daughters. The Lord's disposition toward the suffering is clear. He says, "You must not mistreat any widow or fatherless child. If you do mistreat them, they will no doubt cry to me, and I will certainly hear their cry" (Exodus 22:22–23). Naomi's tears were cherished by the Lord. He didn't turn his face away from them or close his ears or heart to her cries. Knowing this about Naomi's God, it shouldn't surprise us too terribly that the arc of this story is about to bend away from grief toward grace. But it's not quite time for that yet.

As the three widows set out to journey the thirty miles back to Bethlehem, Naomi pleaded with her "daughters" (Ruth 1:11) to leave her, return to their people and their gods, and find husbands for themselves. She had reconciled whatever heart she had left to another painful loss, and then "she kissed them, and wept loudly" (1:9), confessing her despair: "My life is much too bitter for you to share, because the LORD's hand has turned *against me*" (1:13). Poor Naomi didn't know that her God was sharing true life with her; she believed that she herself was under a curse and utterly alone.

Sharing Life Together

At last, a little shaft of light began to break through into Naomi's darkness. Perhaps she wasn't unloved after all. Her beloved daughter-in-law Ruth pledged whatever life and strength she had left to her. Ruth chose not to protect herself from the curse Naomi thought she was under and would instead willingly share in her bitterness. Naomi would not be left alone. Here is Ruth's well-known promise to her mother-in-law: "Don't plead with me to abandon you or to return and not follow you. For wherever you go, I will go, and wherever you live, I will live; your people will be my people, and your God will be my God. Where you die, I will die, and there I will be buried. May the LORD punish me, and do so severely, if anything but death separates you and me" (Ruth 1:16–18).

Through the lips of a cursed Moabite widow, the Lord spoke words of comfort to his brokenhearted daughter. Through this surprising channel, Ruth was the means by which the Lord met

Naomi's needs for food and offspring to carry on the family name. So, "when Naomi saw that Ruth was determined to go with her, she stopped talking to her" (Ruth 1:18). Naomi chose to accept Ruth's extraordinary devotion.

Ruth's determination to stay with Naomi comes from a Hebrew word that denotes "be stout, strong, bold, solid, hard."[9] Ruth resisted Naomi's logical objections and refused to give in to her. In fact, she insisted that she would "commit to die and be buried with Naomi," which "was the greatest possible commitment in the ancient world," a commitment Ruth made willingly.[10] Further, we read in 1:14 that Ruth "clung" to Naomi. This is the same word that is used in Genesis 2:24 to describe the "bond that exists in marriage ... loyalty to a covenant commitment."[11] Ruth was committed to lay down her entire life to serve Naomi, sticking with her no matter what. She would help carry the weight of Naomi's broken heart. Through her, Naomi soon discovered that she was beloved, and surprisingly, she learned that truth through a foreigner.

Call Me Mara

When Naomi and Ruth finally made it back to Bethlehem, the women of the town greeted Naomi by name. Her answer bespoke her heart and even her faith: "'Don't call me Naomi. Call me Mara,' she answered, 'for the Almighty has made me very bitter. I went away full, but the LORD has brought me back empty. Why do you call me Naomi, since the LORD has opposed me, and the Almighty has afflicted me?'" (Ruth 1:20–21). Naomi's first words upon returning to Bethlehem were words of identity.

She had been known as Naomi, which meant "kindness, pleasantness, sweetness." But this name had been stripped from her by what she thought was an exacting, punishing God. The new name she had given herself, Mara, meant "bitter."

We don't know how Naomi felt about leaving Bethlehem in the first place. Perhaps she thought it was a good idea and she went along with Elimelech's plan. Or maybe she thought it wasn't the right choice. She might have even trusted that God would bless her obedience to Elimelech and protect her in exchange. But that's not what happened. In essence, she said: "I left during a famine, though my family was full. I came back in time for the grain harvest, but my life is empty." And she wasn't the only empty one: Ruth had been married for years yet didn't have any children, and now she was a widowed immigrant from a despised nation. Although Ruth seemed empty, she was determined to fill her life with love and care for her mother-in-law.

If you have been following along with the other stories in this book, you are probably thinking that it sounds like a perfect set-up for the Lord. *Things look desperate and hopeless? Great! This is where God enters!* It's easy for those of us who read the whole story to think that Naomi/Mara should have had more faith and not been so down in the dumps. Although she was a daughter of Abraham, the circumstances in her life had taught her that she didn't have any assurance that help was on the way. The thought that she was in fact beloved was laughable to her.

Once they had settled into Naomi's formerly abandoned home, Ruth asked Naomi's permission to go into the barley fields and gather grain after the harvesters. As she went, Ruth just happened upon the field of an honorable man who was also her husband's relative, Boaz. She might have thought her choice was by chance, but Proverbs teaches us, "Even a courageous person's steps are determined by the LORD" (Proverbs 20:24). The Lord's inclining of Ruth's steps into this exact field at this exact time is proof that the Lord was aware of and for both of them. He did no less for Ruth and Naomi than what he asks of his followers: to care for the widow and destitute (see James 1:27).

When Boaz, the owner of the field, saw Ruth working, he asked, "Whose young woman is this?" (Ruth 2:5). He didn't ask, "Who is she?" but rather, "*Whose* is she?" He wanted to know who she belonged to, where her identity was rooted. The response was one that would have shut down most of the men of Bethlehem. "She is the young Moabite woman who returned with Naomi from the territory of Moab" (2:6). *A Moabite woman? A barren widow?* Most men in the town would not have given her another thought.

True Biblical Womanhood

Here's where our story pushes against the stereotypical portrait of femininity that is so common in certain evangelical circles where a meritocracy makes its demands. If biblical womanhood looks like the quintessential Victorian woman, Ruth would be considered an utter failure. Boaz's foreman testified, "She came and has been on her feet since early morning, except that she rested a little in the shelter" (Ruth 2:7). Physically, Ruth was a strong woman, one who was familiar with physical labor under the hot sun. She was no pampered weakling who needed housekeepers to do all the dirty work while she read, practiced the pianoforte, or embroidered. Impressed by her strength and determination, Boaz told Ruth: "Listen, my daughter. Don't go and gather grain in another field, and don't leave this one, but stay here close to my female servants. See which field they are harvesting, and follow them. Haven't I ordered the young men not to touch you? When you are thirsty, go and drink from the jars the young men have filled" (Ruth 2:8–9).

Because Boaz was a "man of noble character" and a man of integrity, he immediately perceived the peril Ruth was in and stepped up to protect and provide for her. Boaz had the power and resources necessary to care for the poor and powerless. Rather than see her as an outsider, he called her "daughter," "a very affectionate term to use for a foreigner."[12] In response, Ruth "fell facedown, bowed to the ground, and said to him, 'Why have I found favor with you, so that you notice me, although I am a foreigner?'" (Ruth 2:10)

Ruth saw herself as the unloved outsider. But Boaz saw her as more than that. He saw her as a virtuous woman, one who had put aside her own interests to share the life of her broken and needy mother-in-law. It was this quality in Ruth that resonated with Boaz, because he was just like her. He put aside his own profit for the sake of a stranger. Like Ruth, Boaz was also a person who had "come for refuge" (2:12) under the wings of the Lord God of Israel. Seeking refuge under the protective covering of the Lord is a common theme in the prayers in Psalms:

> Protect me as the pupil of your eye;
> hide me in the shadow of your wings. (Psalm 17:8)

> Be gracious to me, God, be gracious to me,
> for I take refuge in you.
> I will seek refuge in the shadow of your wings
> until danger passes. (Psalm 57:1; see also 63:7)

Also, like Ruth was for Naomi, Boaz was for Ruth a channel of grace. Boaz "comforted and encouraged" her (Ruth 2:13), even though she was different from the other women. Ruth had come to the Lord to find security and asylum, and Boaz was the avenue that the Lord employed for his blessing. Boaz prayed that the Lord would reward Ruth for her backbreaking faithfulness to Naomi, and it was Boaz himself who answered this prayer. He instructed his servants to provide for Ruth and cautioned the men not to harass or attack her while she gleaned. Boaz acted as her refuge and provided abundantly for her and Naomi.

When Ruth returned home after gleaning the fields and meeting Boaz, Naomi ascertained who it was who had protected and provided for them, and she began to realize that the Lord had "not *abandoned his kindness* to the living or the dead" (Ruth 2:20). The woman who once referred to herself as Mara, the one whom the Almighty had made bitter and empty, the one whom the Lord opposed and afflicted, was now beginning to see that she was actually *beloved*. As the seven weeks went on for the barley and wheat harvests, Naomi's faith that God might in fact care about her began to grow again. He was reminding her that he was a God of kindness and grace, and he continued to reveal this to her in ways she could have never imagined.

The Odd Couple

Because he was a man of wealth and stature in the community, it would be easy to miss that Boaz had his own ignominious heritage. Yes, Ruth was a cursed Moabite, someone who would never be allowed in Israel's worship, but Boaz's mother was Rahab, the prostitute from Jericho (see Matthew 1:5), which might explain why this upstanding landowner was still a bachelor. Every resident in Rahab's city, aside from her and her family, had been annihilated by the conquering Israelites. Her salvation from destruction literally hung by a thread (Joshua 2:17). And though she had been sheltered from destruction, like Ruth, her former life was utterly gone. Without the willingness of a son of Israel to take her into his home, she would have floundered. Boaz's mother knew what it was to lose everything and to face great need. She was probably glad to find refuge from the destruction that had come on Jericho and become part of the family of a man who was willing to take her into his home. Boaz learned about caring for outcast women from his father.

Soon, Naomi devised a way for both she and Ruth to be cared for. At the end of the barley harvest, when Boaz and all of his workers winnowed the grain and spent the night in the field, Ruth was to propose marriage to him. Naomi told Ruth to wash, anoint, dress herself appropriately, and find the place where he slept after the harvest party. She was to go and lie down beside him and uncover his feet. This would demonstrate to Boaz that she wanted to marry him. So Ruth waited until midnight, after the feasting had ended, and found where Boaz slept. Here's the passage:

At midnight, Boaz was startled, turned over, and there lying at his feet was a woman! So he asked, "Who are you?"

"I am Ruth, your servant," she replied. "Take me under your wing, for you are a family redeemer."

Then he said, "May the Lord bless you, my daughter. You have shown more kindness now than before, because you have not pursued younger men, whether rich or poor. Now don't be afraid, my daughter. I will do for you whatever you say, since all the people in my town know that you are a woman of noble character. Yes, it is true that I am a family redeemer, but there is a redeemer closer than I am. Stay here tonight, and in the morning, if he wants to redeem you, that's good. Let him redeem you. But if he doesn't want to redeem you, as the Lord lives, I will. Now lie down until morning."

So she lay down at his feet until morning but got up while it was still dark. Then Boaz said, "Don't let it be known that a woman came to the threshing floor." And he told Ruth, "Bring the shawl you're wearing and hold it out." When she held it out, he shoveled six measures of barley into her shawl, and she went into the town. (Ruth 3:8–15)

In the same way that Ruth had sought refuge under the wings of the Lord, she now sought it under the cloak of Boaz. She needed to be protected and provided for; she needed a commitment from him to be married. And she wasn't too timid to ask for it.

When Ruth asked Boaz to cover her with his cloak, she was proposing marriage, and the act of covering her was analogous to giving her an engagement ring. She didn't wait for him to initiate the relationship. And he knew the kind of woman she was: strong, courageous, determined, and bold. Rather than portray her as a paragon of Victorian femininity, we see her courageous character: how she refused to take the easy road, leave Naomi, and return to her Moabite roots. She worked hard and carried many pounds of grain home to feed her mother-in-law. She labored for at least seven weeks in this way. When Naomi instructed her to go to Boaz, Ruth did more than just show up. She proposed marriage: "I am Ruth, your servant. ... Take me under your wing" (Ruth 3:9). And Boaz happily responded to her proposal: "Now don't be afraid, my daughter. I will do for you whatever you say. ... I know that you are a woman of noble character" (Ruth 3:11).

Boaz wasn't confused by any sort of Victorian stereotype of femininity either. He had learned all he needed to know about women who didn't exactly fit the mold from his mother, Rahab. He knew Ruth had a heart for God and a love for her family. He knew she was a woman of integrity. So, he promised to protect her reputation and to settle the matter of marriage that day. Then he gave her "six measures of barley," which amounted to eighty pounds to carry home to Naomi. Don't think about Ruth as the title character from *Sleeping Beauty*; think of her more as Luisa from *Encanto*. That was exactly the kind of woman Naomi and Boaz needed.

Soon Boaz handled the legal hurdle that might have thwarted their plan, and the marriage was set. Boaz declared that he was taking Ruth to be his wife. The people and the elders of the city who heard him invoked their blessing on the marriage. "May the LORD make the woman who is entering your house like Rachel and Leah, who together built the house of Israel. ... May your house become like the house of Perez, the son Tamar bore to Judah" (Ruth 4:11–12).

Notice the names of the women they hoped Ruth would be like: Rachel, the beautiful but idolatrous deceiver; the unloved and unattractive Leah; and Tamar, the unloved, abused woman who feigned prostitution to become the mother of Perez by Judah. Boaz's mother, Rahab the prostitute, was also part of the beloved genealogy.

This story tells us that *anyone*, and I mean *anyone*, who flees to the Lord for refuge and looks to him for protection and provision is beloved. And this promise isn't just for women. It's also for men who think that it's too late for them, who, perhaps like Boaz, think that work is all they'll ever have.

At Last

If you are a beautiful, young, willowy woman, that's great. Throw yourself on the mercy of the Lord. If you have always thought of yourself as unattractive, too big, too loud, too strong, or too bold: throw yourself on the mercy of the Lord. If you're a divorcee or a widow, someone who thinks you have made too many mistakes to ever turn your life around now, if you have been abused for years and have finally extricated yourself from that deception and danger, you too can throw yourself on the mercy of the Lord.

If you are a man who has watched life pass him by, who has found himself alone and wondering whether all the hours he has spent in his career or hobbies are really the entire measure of his identity, surrender it all to Christ. If you are a man who doesn't want to get married or who likes spending evenings reading, painting, and playing music, throw yourself on the mercy of the Lord. In all of our uniqueness, quirkiness, individuality, and brokenness, we can ask him to cover us with his cloak, or—to change the metaphor—to cover us with his wings as we hide from the attack of our enemies or even from our own voices of despair. We don't have to look like anyone else's definition of masculinity or femininity. All those stereotypes belong in the identity-crushing meritocracy. Whether you are a Ruth or a Boaz, a Rachel or a Leah, a Tamar or a Judah, flee to him, and Jesus will throw his cloak over you.

As this beautiful story progresses, we find Ruth and Boaz marrying, and eventually Ruth gave birth to a baby boy, Obed. When Naomi took this long-awaited grandson onto her lap, her neighbors rejoiced: "The neighbor women said, 'A son has been born to Naomi,' and they named him Obed. He was the father of Jesse, the father of David" (Ruth 4:17).

At last, Naomi's arms were filled with the grandbaby she had longed for. At last, Boaz had a virtuous, strong wife. And at last, Ruth had a protector who loved and honored her, and a son to raise. Obed went on to have a son, Jesse, and Jesse's future son became the most honored king in all of Israel, David. What amazing grace is showered on the bereft, the outcast, and the empty.

The Real Love Story

The real love story in this book is not about Boaz and Ruth. The real love story is behind the scenes. It is the love of God for his straying sheep. Elimelech and Naomi made unwise, perhaps even disobedient, choices. They suffered great loss. But, right when it seemed that all hope was lost, God's love for the unloved broke in, and through the strangest of sources: a Moabite woman and the son of a prostitute. As Old Testament scholar and pastor Iain Duguid writes, "Grace is always God's last word."[13]

The wonderful news from Ruth's story is that "in Christ, God comes running to meet us."[14] The Lord had not left bitter Naomi without a redeemer. Yes, in this story we see loss and heartache, but we also see a God who runs to the aid of the weak and poor. And where baby Obed renewed and sustained Naomi in her old age, the Lord Jesus comes to us all, young and old, isolated or surrounded by family, with promises to protect and keep us always, for he has said, "I will never leave you or abandon you. Therefore, we may boldly say, The Lord is my helper, I will not be afraid. What can man do to me?" (Hebrews 13:5–6).

The book of Ruth is in the Bible because the Lord wants us to understand his love for disobedient insiders and disreputable outsiders. It reminds us that God has a gracious plan to redeem, a plan that nothing can thwart. It exists for those who have trouble seeing past their loss and confusion. It is there because we, like Noami, Ruth, and Boaz, are God's beloved. The stereotypes valued and imposed in a meritocracy are demolished by the grace of God for those who wrongly assume that it's too late for them. Aged Naomi, mature Boaz, and the childless widow all find a place under the Lord's covering.

Digging Deeper

1. What messages have you heard about what it means to be biblically feminine or masculine? How do these messages clash with the message of Ruth?

2. Have you ever felt that because you didn't fit the popular mold these messages portray, you were somehow out of step? If so, how?

3. What does the story of Naomi, Ruth, and Boaz tell you about the people God loves to bless?

4. Not every story ends with such blessing and joy. Can you think of any portions of the Bible where you might find the assurance that the love that the Lord showed them, he shows us, too? If so, where?

5. Summarize what you've learned in this chapter in four or five sentences.

7

David and Bathsheba

Imagine you just discovered that someone had been slandering you, dragging your name through the mud, or saying things about you that simply were not true. Or, maybe the things they said were true (in a certain perspective) but were private and needed an explanation that others weren't entitled to. Now, imagine that this denigration had been done online. Picture opening up Facebook or X (formerly known as Twitter) to discover that someone had uncovered the worst thing you've ever done (or been accused of doing) and posted it for trillions of eyes to see. How would you respond?

Public shaming is nothing new. In the past, guilty parties might have found themselves shackled in the public square, perhaps pelted with rotten vegetables, or worse. In 1850, Nathaniel Hawthorne chronicled what today we would call clergy sexual abuse in *The Scarlet Letter.* Hawthorne tells the story of Hester Prynne, who was seduced by her clergyman, then sentenced to shame and ignominy, forced to wear a red *A*, and tell everyone she was an adulteress.

Names and reputations matter. They live on—sometimes for thousands of years. Two of the women we've considered, Gomer and Tamar, have names linked to the infamous description "prostitute." One had a name that was analogous to failure; another had a name that was never uttered by her owner, though she had the privilege of naming God. We've considered Noami, a woman whose life was so ruined that she changed her name to reflect her loss, while her daughter-in-law's good reputation paved the way for her blessing. Think of it. Thousands of years after these people lived, they still bear their reputation. Reputations matter: "A good name is to be chosen over great wealth" (Proverbs 22:1; see also Ecclesiastes 7:1).

What does your name mean to you? Have you ever experienced the unjustified tarnishing of it? What was that like? How has the shame of a ruined reputation affected you? What if you were wrongly accused for thousands of years by women and men who were supposed to be part of your family?

There are women in the Bible whose good names have been unjustifiably tarnished. We've already looked at some of them: Sarah, Hagar, Tamar. What other women could you mention? In this chapter, we're going to consider another woman whose reputation has consistently been besmirched by the church. Her name is analogous with women who seem disgraceful and therefore unloved by God. The biased way that her story has been told might make us assume that she'd never be included in the family of faith. We're considering her now because, in truth, she's not unloved. We need to declare that she is our beloved sister, and we need to speak the truth about her.

Godly Women, Ruined Reputations

Adultery—a word that conjures up images of deception, treachery, and, for some, personal memories of heartache. Maybe your memories flow from childhood, with parents who warred against each other and eventually divorced. Perhaps you remember the tearing apart of your world as accusations pierced your once peaceful home, and arguments ensued about schedules and what house you'd live in and when. Adultery tears apart families. But it can also leave a shattered reputation, especially for a woman. Few labels ruin a reputation the way that "adulterous woman" does.

I assume that not one of my readers has been unscathed by the terrible woe of adultery, considering that in the United States, "approximately half of people in married relationships cheat at least one time during the course of the marriage."[15] None of us are strangers to the heartbreak, loss, and broken promises caused by adultery.

Bathsheba and Her Scarlet Letter

Remember how I asked you about people with ruined reputations in Scripture? Whom did you name? If I were to ask you to name one adulterous couple in the Bible, my guess is that David and Bathsheba would pretty quickly come to mind. They have long been depicted as the classic adulterous pair. And, considering the devastation that their families experienced, we see how adultery always carries consequences far beyond the mere sexual act. What I'd like you to do now, though, is to reconsider the definition of the word "adultery."

It is described as "voluntary sexual intercourse." I want you to notice that word "voluntary," and I want to ask you: *Did Bathsheba have a choice?* Was her liaison with David *voluntary*? Did she tempt or seduce him? Was what happened between them actually an adulterous affair, or was it something far more sinister?

Like Hester Prynne in Nathaniel Hawthorne's *The Scarlet Letter*, Bathsheba has a reputation as the woman who tempted a good man to sin. Her reputation was ruined. She is the quintessential seductress. But, is this besmirching of her name justified? Here is the first description we read of Bathsheba, from 2 Samuel 11:1–5:

> In the spring when kings march out to war, David sent Joab with his officers and all Israel. They destroyed the Ammonites and besieged Rabbah, but David remained in Jerusalem.
>
> One evening David got up from his bed and strolled around on the roof of the palace. From the roof he saw a woman bathing—a very beautiful woman. So David sent someone to inquire about her, and he said, "Isn't this Bathsheba, daughter of Eliam and wife of Uriah the Hethite?"
>
> David sent messengers to get her, and when she came to him, he slept with her. Now she had just been purifying herself from her uncleanness. Afterward, she returned home. The woman conceived and sent word to inform David, "I am pregnant."

After David was thwarted in his scheme to get Bathsheba's husband to have sex with her so that his part in her pregnancy would remain hidden, David arranged for Uriah's murder on the battlefield. Scripture describes Bathsheba's response to her husband's death this way: "When Uriah's wife heard that her husband, Uriah, had died, she mourned for him. When the time of mourning ended, David had her brought to his house. She became his wife and bore him a son. However, the LORD considered what David had done to be evil" (2 Samuel 11:26–27).

Ruining a Good Woman's Reputation

Bathsheba is frequently painted as the woman who brought down the righteous King David. She is continually referred to in books, commentaries, and sermons as "Bathsheba, the adulteress." As commentator Richard D. Phillips writes, she is also used as an example of the dangers of immodesty: "David's sin with Bathsheba does offer women lessons regarding sexual modesty."[16]

Further examples from a book on preaching by John Bisagno portrays Bathsheba as culpable: "While David had committed adultery and murder, and had been involved in a cover-up that made Watergate look like a grade school play, he repented and made a decision to serve the Lord. We are left to ponder whether Bathsheba repented, as well."[17] *Sure, David was sinful,* this author admits, *but at least he repented. Not so sure about Bathsheba, though.* But this author's conclusion begs the question: What was Bathsheba's sin? We are not told of her repentance, but perhaps that is because she was a victim, not an adulteress. The

Bible doesn't say that she did anything evil. In fact, it says, "The LORD considered what David had done to be evil" (2 Samuel 11:27). Scripture is silent about any culpability on Bathsheba's part. But that doesn't stop certain commentators from continuing to ruin her good name.

If you're like me, you've probably heard this story dozens of times, and Bathsheba is almost always portrayed as the seductive nude, waiting for some man to notice her. After all, she is the one who put on the rooftop porn show, or so we're told. Despite this repeated description of her character, the idea that she was bathing on the roof of her house is actually due to a translation error. Further, even though the Holy Spirit doesn't tell us, some readers propound, "It could also be assumed that Bathsheba may have been aware of David's interest in her before he called for her to come over to the palace."[18] Why should that be assumed about her? The text tells us that she is a righteous woman who loved her husband and mourned deeply for him. But another commentator even proposes, "As spontaneous and undisciplined as this liaison sounds, in fact it was probably an affair that developed over a much longer period of time."[19] Why are we asked by those who stringently insist on not adding to Scripture or making assumptions not strictly dictated by the text to assume that there was previous collusion? If David had already had a dalliance with Bathsheba, why did he have to ask her identity? Another author suggests, "Although the blame for adultery is placed squarely upon David, Bathsheba apparently does not discourage the illicit relationship."[20] Why do we assume that she encouraged the relationship?

Here's another example of the besmirching of her character, "He ordered her to be brought to him, and he 'lay with her' (2 Samuel 11:4), apparently with her consent. This evidently went on for a while, and in time she found that she was pregnant. By the law of the time, adultery meant death for the woman."[21] Why does Richard Losch, the commentator, assume her "consent"? David was a man who commanded the entire nation, and to resist his will would have been punishable by death. On more than eight different occasions in this narrative, we are told that David commanded significant action:

- David *sent* Joab with his officers and all Israel to war (2 Samuel 11:1).

- David *sent* an unnamed person to try to discover Bathsheba's identity (2 Samuel 11:3).

- David *sent* messengers to "get" her (2 Samuel 11:4). The word "get" doesn't mean that he just sent a party bus for her. Rather, it means, to "take, grasp, seize; accept, receive; fetch, bring; take away, remove" her from her home.[22]

- David *sent* orders to Joab who *sent* Uriah to him (2 Samuel 11:6).

- David got Uriah drunk so that Uriah would compromise his commitments (2 Samuel 11:13).

- Chillingly, David *sent* a letter commanding Uriah's execution by his own hand to Joab (2 Samuel 11:14).

- After Bathsheba had completed her time of mourning for Uriah, David "had her *brought* to his house" (2 Samuel 11:27). Note that the word translated "brought" here is different from the word translated "get" or "take" in verse 4.

From the prophet Nathan's confrontation of David, here is how David is described:

- He was a rich man with very large flocks and herds (2 Samuel 12:1).
- The rich man "took" the poor man's beloved lone sheep (2 Samuel 12:4).
- David "took" the wife of Uriah (2 Samuel 12:10). Remember that "took" means to "take, grasp, seize; accept, receive; fetch, bring; take away, remove."

Not one word in this entire narrative demands, or even insinuates, that Bathsheba instigated or, much less, voluntarily complied with David's designs on her. Certainly, if Bathsheba had been complicit, Nathan, the prophet who rebuked David, would have called her out, too. And she wouldn't have been the innocent lamb in Nathan's parable. Nathan's confrontation in the power of the Holy Spirit certainly doesn't say anything that should cause us to assume that this was anything other than an abuse of power by a spoiled, bored, absolutely powerful man. So, why is the denigration of Bathsheba such a consistent refrain? Why is she so unloved by the church?

Furthermore, why do some commentators insist that this was not a one-off rape but rather an ongoing affair? Perhaps it is because they don't understand a woman's physiology and can't fathom that Bathsheba might have gotten pregnant after only one encounter with David. Perhaps they don't know that a woman usually becomes fertile and ovulates anywhere from days 11–21 after the first day of her previous period. In addition, sperm can survive up to five days in a woman's body. Scripture reveals that Bathsheba was cleansing herself at the end of her menstrual cycle (2 Samuel 11:4). The fact is, the Bible tells us that Bathsheba had just finished her period, so it was entirely possible for her to become pregnant at that time. Moreover, this means that David's abusive encounter with her could have, from a biological perspective, resulted in pregnancy. Even so, theologians and commentators continue to misrepresent the text. One commentator even assumes that Bathsheba was cleansing herself *after* having sex with David: "When [Bathsheba] came to him—apparently voluntarily—he lay with her. Bathsheba *'purified herself of her uncleanness'* and then returned to her house."[23]

Yes, apparently, Bathsheba did come to David when he sent for her, but what does that mean? Could a woman refuse a king's wishes? Furthermore, the text doesn't state that she cleansed herself *after* having sex with David. Rather, she cleansed herself after her menstrual cycle, and this is what she was doing when David first saw her and set his designs on her.

Despite all of this textual evidence supporting Bathsheba's innocence, commentators go even further in condemning her. One well-respected leader speaks about David's abuse of Bathsheba as something to be envied: "And since David was the king, he could do what most men can only dream of doing. If he wanted a woman, he could take her, and so he did: 'Then David sent messengers to get her. She came to him, and he slept with her' (v. 4a)."[24]

Do "most men" really "dream of" forcefully taking any woman they want? If that is the perspective of "most men," it is no wonder that Bathsheba's reputation has been so tarnished. Perhaps she has been objectified by many because objectifying women is considered normal. It really is no wonder that Bathsheba's story is so misunderstood and confused. Some commentators even say that the death of David and Bathsheba's baby is, at least in part, a judgment on Bathsheba for her role in the "affair."

Not all commentators insist that Bathsheba was ultimately at fault, but even so, they often propose that she should have been able to resist, as "far as is possible." Women today are morally responsible for maintaining their sexual purity *so far as is possible*. But there is no evidence that Bathsheba deliberately placed herself in this situation, and the Bible's blame lies squarely on David.

Gladly, here we find commentators like David Turner and Darrell Bock, who get it right: "The Old Testament account of Bathsheba's adultery with David (2 Sam 11) appears to characterize her as the passive victim of his aggression."[25]

David's Harem Wasn't Enough

David already had six wives. He also undoubtedly had numerous concubines. If he had been bored or lonely one evening, he didn't need to spend the hours pining away. There were many sexual options open to him. David's sexual sin is not precipitated by a need for sex. He is the rich man in Nathan's parable, having access to all the women he could possibly want. David's actions were not even precipitated by the desire to look at a pretty woman. He was rich with wives and concubines. David's desire for Bathsheba was not a desire for sex. It was a desire to exercise power and experience conquest. Instead of going out in conquest of Israel's enemies as he should have, David gave into the temptation to stay home. It was the time of year "when kings march out to war," but instead of joining his comrades in bravery, he decided to express his impulse to conquer in another way. He used his power over life and death to conquer another man's beloved wife. There is a reason the book of Samuel begins the story in this way. Instead of warring against his enemies, David warred against his faithful servant Uriah, his wife, his own family, and ultimately his own soul.

Bathsheba's Reputation according to the Bible

Let's look at the words the Spirit uses to describe Bathsheba in the opening of this story:

- She was "very beautiful" (2 Samuel 11:2).

- She was a wife and a daughter (2 Samuel 11:3).

- She was obedient to the law about ritual cleansing after her period (2 Samuel 11:4).

- The only words in this narrative that we hear her say are, "I am pregnant" (2 Samuel 11:5).

- She deeply mourned for days for her husband Uriah (2 Samuel 11:26–27).

How does the prophet Nathan describe Bathsheba? He tells a story about a rich man who had more than he could ever need, and a poor man with one cherished little lamb:

> There were two men in a certain city, one rich and the other poor. The rich man had very large flocks and herds, but the poor man had nothing except one small ewe lamb that he had bought. He raised her, and she grew up with him and with his children. From his meager food she would eat, from his cup she would drink, and in his arms she would sleep. She was like a daughter to him. (2 Samuel 12:1–3)

Bethsheba had been "raised" and "grew up" with Uriah's family. In Nathan's parable, Uriah fed her by hand, and she would drink from his cup. Bathsheba would sleep "in his arms." She was beloved like a daughter to him (2 Samuel 12:3).

Do these descriptions of Bathsheba's relationship with Uriah sound like she would have been out hustling for an illicit liaison with the king her husband served? Certainly, if that's true, the Holy Spirit, who speaks all the truth that we need to rightly understand, wouldn't have portrayed Bathsheba in this way.

David eventually comforts Bathsheba (2 Samuel 12:24) after the loss of her husband and their baby. To "comfort" Bathsheba meant that he felt empathy for her, as he should have, particularly because of the deaths he occasioned in her life. She mourned for her husband and for her little baby, who lived only seven days. As Bathsheba's story progressed, she took her place as one of David's wives and eventually gave birth to Solomon.

Bathsheba, Innocent and Wise

We're not told anything more about Bathsheba until David was dying and a struggle for the throne ensued. Here, we learn more about the character of Bathsheba and her relationship with David. The prophet Nathan informed her that Solomon's elder half-brother, Adonijah, had declared himself to be king. Apparently, Bathsheba was unaware of the danger that she and her son were in. Nathan advised her to go to the king, and we learn a wonderful new truth about Bathsheba: at some point, David made a promise to her that her son, Solomon, would reign after him. Perhaps she pressed him for a promise that she and any future offspring would be protected instead of relegated to insignificance. She wanted her son to have a secure place of prominence so she wouldn't become "that woman" who tempted the king to sin. David's promise was known to Nathan the prophet, who advised Bathsheba to remind David of it. David responded to her: "As the Lord lives, who has redeemed my life from every difficulty, just as I swore to you by the Lord God of Israel: Your son Solomon is to become king after me, and he is the one who is to sit on my throne in my place, that is exactly what I will do this very day" (1 Kings 1:29–30). Soon Solomon was declared king, and Bathsheba became the queen mother.

The final vignette we're given of Bathsheba is when the usurper, Adonijah, asked her to request that David's concubine, Abishag, be given to him as a wife (1 Kings 2:13–22). Bathsheba approached her son, Solomon, and made Adonijah's request. Once again, she was unaware of the danger that such a request would put her in. But Solomon understood what Adonijah's request really meant and had him executed.

What do we learn about Bathsheba from these two stories? First of all, we learn that, at some point, she was wise enough to extract from David a promise that her son, Solomon, would reign. She wouldn't be discarded or treated with disdain after David's death. But we also learn something from her request on behalf of Adonijah. We learn that she was perhaps naive, an innocent who took requests at face value and didn't assume the worst about people. Maybe this helps us understand why she came to David that fateful night so many years ago. It's not besmirching her reputation to say that she wasn't the sort of person who indulged in intrigue or assumed the worst about people. When David took her from her home, why would she automatically assume that her king and husband's commander had something nefarious planned? Similarly, while Adonijah was plotting to become king, Bathsheba wasn't aware of his impure motives; all she knew was that he wanted one of David's concubines. With this context in mind, we could consider reframing her reputation from a wicked seductress sporting a scarlet letter to an innocent woman who assumed good motives. She was beautiful, and maybe she thought everyone else was, too.

Don't misunderstand. I don't mean that she was stupid or a ditzy airhead. I mean that she may have been one of those people for whom the world is filled with good people, doing good things, for good reasons. Maybe she was one of those people that Paul writes about: "To the pure, everything is pure" (Titus 1:15). To the pure, clean, and innocent, everything is pure, clean, and innocent. Her honorable king required her presence? Of course, she would respond! Adonijah wanted to marry Abishag? Of course, she would help! She never seemed to see the potential evil behind people's requests.

Is Bathsheba a character we would consider unloved? Well, she certainly has been by the church. In sermons, history books, and commentaries, she has been denigrated for centuries by those who have automatically assumed that her bathing (in obedience to the ritual laws of cleanness) was meant to lure a good man into her evil clutches. She stands with every other sexually assaulted woman, especially those in the church, who assumed that the sweet youth pastor or beloved shepherd was calling her into his office because he loved her as a brother loves a sister.

Bathsheba and #ChurchToo

One in four women have been sexually assaulted; many of them have also been blamed for their assault. Women in the church have been cast as vixens who "asked for it." Many victims of abuse have not been believed or have been silenced through shame and intimidation. The recent report about the prior leadership of the Southern Baptist Convention's shameful complicity in disbelieving women and covering up for men's sins against them is instructive,[26] yet it's just the tip of the iceberg.

The story of Bathsheba can speak to the abused. Bathsheba's story can speak to assaulted and accused women about the ability of God to turn deep grief and loss into a life of blessing, even to including her in the genealogy of the Son. For this is where we hear Bathsheba's name mentioned next: in the New Testament, as part of the bloodline of the promised Son who was also a King. Here she is referred to as "Uriah's wife" (Matthew 1:6), because the Spirit wants to remind us about David's sin against two innocents, Uriah *and* Bathsheba, and their role in bringing forth the One who redeems both the innocent and the scheming.

Jesus knows what it is to have one's reputation attacked when seeking to be obedient to God's commands. Because he lived it, he knows how to sustain women who face the same thing. Beautiful Bathsheba is our sister who, like others before her, experienced the tarnishing of her name on earth and yet will be beloved by God forever.

In this time of #MeToo and #ChurchToo it is imperative that we get this right. If we continue to discount women's stories of abuse, if we continue to paint pictures of wronged women in the Bible as vixens instead of sisters, if we assume that every man's sexual sin must be a woman's fault, or that *all women are seductresses out to ruin good men*, I fear the church will lose this generation of women.

Perhaps we could finally bring an end to disrespecting women just because they're women, starting with Bathsheba. Perhaps we could finally come to the place where we see our sisters, especially those who have been victims of abuse, as beloved, treasured, highly desired, and beautiful jewels in the hand of the Lord.

We're All So Inconsistent

One final thought about the way we view people like David and Bathsheba: It is really easy to categorize others as being either all good or all bad. Instead, we must learn to see them as the complex beings they are: sometimes full of faith and other times overflowing with sin.

In sharing Bathsheba's story and trying to correct some of the misinformation that persists about her, I don't mean to propose that she was sinless. Of course, she wasn't. Obviously, I don't believe that she deserves the bad reputation she's been given. Aside from Eve, Bathsheba is probably the biblical figure most denigrated in the church. Just like everyone, she needed God's forgiveness, but she also lived with great faith and wisdom, as a beloved daughter of God.

David, of course, is thought of as one of our beloved heroes of faith: he slew Goliath, he sang worship to God, and he ruled righteously. He was a "man after [God's] own heart" (1 Samuel 13:14), *but he also failed in dreadful and destructive ways*. Sadly, he faced many years of trouble because of his sin, but he also had seasons of ruling the nation in faithfulness. Yet, he knew God's forgiveness after his repentance.

In looking at both David and Bathsheba as sinner-saints, it is good to recognize them as both unloved and beloved: seemingly unloved because of their sin and others' sins against them, and yet beloved because the Lord loves all who come to him in faith, no matter their reputation.

The Joy of Repentance and Forgiveness

Can anything good come out of such a terrible story? Were Bathsheba and David actually beloved by the Lord? For thousands of years, Christians have taken David's prayer, recorded in Psalm 51, as a source of great comfort when faced with their own failures. The psalm begins with this opening: "A psalm of David, when the prophet Nathan came to him after he had gone to Bathsheba."

Once David recognized his wicked culpability and self-righteousness, he begged the Lord for forgiveness. Notice again that this sin is laid completely at David's feet. "He had gone to Bathsheba." But notice also that David relied on the very attributes of God that we can rely on too: God's graciousness, his faithful love, and abundant compassion (Psalm 51:1). He knew that the Lord was the only one who could cleanse him from his sin against the woman who had been obediently cleansing herself. He confessed his rebellious acts and that he *alone* was guilty. He cried out to be purified and longed for his joy and gladness to be restored. He knew that he needed a clean heart and a steadfast spirit. He begged God to help him remember the joy of the salvation he knew in the past, and he prayed for release from "the guilt of bloodshed" (51:14). He was a rapist and a murderer, and he had finally come to know it. Now he needed assurance of forgiveness. And in God's kindness, and because of the perfect obedience of Jesus in his substitutionary death, David was granted forgiveness and grace and was restored to joy once again, although there were temporal consequences in his family.

He Took Our Reputation and Granted Us His Good Name

Jesus is the only one who has ever loved women and men perfectly, the way they should be loved: seeing both the darkness and the beauty of their souls and longing for their complete wholeness and joy. Jesus is the conqueror who willingly laid down his life on the cross for the rapist and the murderer, for the one who lusted and hated in his heart (Matthew 5:21, 27). He tasted what it means to bear the bitter weight of guilt for deception, the abuse of power, and the theft of sexual assault. He took on the reputation of cursed sinners (2 Corinthians 5:21; Galatians 3:13) so that we might bear his name: beloved, obedient son.

Jesus is the only truly faithful Husband on earth. He is the only righteous King who needs no cleansing but instead pours out his blood for us. He is all we need. If we lived in a meritocracy, King David would certainly have been dethroned. But instead we have been rescued from "the domain of darkness and transferred ... into the kingdom of the Son he loves. In him we have redemption, the forgiveness of sins" (Colossians 1:13–14). We have a generous and gracious King who welcomes David and Bathsheba and the rest of us into his kingdom.

Digging Deeper

1. How often do you think about your reputation? How do you hope you are perceived?

2. Have you ever faced a time when your reputation was tarnished (justly or unjustly)? How did that affect you?

3. How have you thought about Bathsheba in the past? How have you thought about David? How has this chapter challenged those ideas?

4. Read Psalm 51. What does David's repentance teach you? How does it encourage you?

5. It is challenging to see people as complex, not fitting perfectly into either a good or bad box. It is a challenge to see ourselves this way, too. What are some truths from Scripture that can guide the way we view ourselves and one another?

6. Summarize what you learned in this chapter in four or five sentences.

8

And Yet ...

After spending so much time with women and men whose flannelgraph-inappropriate stories have been memorialized in Scripture, it's hard to synthesize them with the common messages rife in much of the twenty-first-century Western church:

> Speak words of faith and you'll magically have all you could ever desire!
>
> Be obedient and you will receive a life of blessing in return!
>
> Be great parents and ...
>
> Be properly masculine or feminine and ...
>
> Vote for the right people and ...

It's hard to fathom how the messages of "work hard," "do good," and "earn your way into God's favor" could claim to find their origin in the same book that records story after story of people of faith who endured endless suffering. And not only did many of them suffer, but many were also denigrated for their faith.

As we have seen, not one of them was perfect, not by a long shot. But they did believe (imperfectly) as they walked faithfully toward that city that Abraham saw: "a city that has foundations, whose architect and builder is God" (Hebrews 11:10). Abraham's reputation is that he "obeyed and set out for a place that he was going to receive as an inheritance. He went out, even though he did not know where he was going. By faith he stayed as a foreigner in the land of promise, living in tents" (Hebrews 11:8–9).

Even though he obeyed, God did not "give him an inheritance in it—not even a foot of ground" (Acts 7:5). *Not even a foot of ground*, though he had faithfully obeyed. Yet he is remembered as the "father of our faith" (see Romans 4:11–12). How could this ever make sense in a meritocracy, where faith, obedience, and merit are said to trump grace? It can't.

By faith, Sarah herself, "received power to conceive" the promised son (Hebrews 11:11). That certainly wouldn't make sense in a meritocracy, would it? How is that fair? How is that right? She laughed in unbelief at God's promise. She forced her slave into her husband's bed. Even after she was finally given the son she had longed for and laughed with joy, she was still an abusive and hard-hearted person who struggled with unbelief and failure.

Hagar, her powerless Egyptian slave, was forced to have sex with aged Abraham, ran away from the abuse of Sarah twice, and twice was met by the Lord at a well in the desert. And yet ... she, the runaway, abused outcast, was the first person to assign a name to him, El Roi, the God who both sees and hears the outcast.

Sarah's promised son, Isaac, fathered Jacob, who had faith in God's promises but was a deceiver, a terrible father, and the cause of immense heartache for all his children, especially Judah. Judah gave up the faith of the family and moved away after selling his baby brother into slavery. There he married a foreigner, tried to silence his wounded conscience, raised two sons who were so wicked God killed them, had sex with his bereaved and deceived daughter-in-law, Tamar, and sentenced her to death, but through her wisdom and courage was finally given grace to repent and woke up from his guilt to proclaim her "righteous."

Tamar, the courageous unloved beloved, has been denigrated by the church when she is the only woman in the Old Testament that is actually called righteous. Again, this is not because she was the only righteous one but because we are tempted to call her anything but. Dressing up as a hooker doesn't seem like an act of faith that would be blessed by God. And yet ...

Naomi followed her husband, Elimilech, into the land of Moab to try to find food, where she was bereaved of her husband and both her sons. In unbelief, she journeyed back to Bethlehem with her gentile daughter-in-law, Ruth, without a testimony of faith, proclaiming that God had made her life "very bitter." "I went away full," she said, "but the Lord has brought me back empty. ... The Lord has opposed me, and the Almighty has afflicted me" (Ruth 1:20–21). If Naomi had been living in a meritocracy (as she supposed), this faithless speech of hers should have eventuated in God's judgment. But that's not what she received. Instead, she was graced with a loving, strong, faithful gentile daughter-in-law and kinsman-redeemer who graced her with a baby to cuddle on her lap, and who has been forever immortalized as the ancestor of the greatest of Israel's human kings as well as Jesus, the King of kings. What did Naomi deserve? What would she have earned in a meritocracy? Destruction and judgment. What did she receive? Blessing upon blessing. Strong Ruth, gracious Boaz, and little baby Obed surrounded a woman who, just like us, was frail, unbelieving, unloved, and yet beloved. And yet ...

Her ancestor, King David, began his journey as a man of courage and faith but soon degenerated into a rapist and murderer. We have a terrible time calling him that because we want to believe that he earned the title "a man after God's own heart," when the truth is that this title was all of grace. And what of our dear sister Bathsheba? Although her reputation has been defiled and destroyed and the church has often portrayed her as unworthy of love, the biblical record actually shows us a woman of courage and wisdom who righteously believed the best about the men in her life. Why is David always lifted up as such a paragon of faith whom we are to follow while Bathsheba is so universally disrespected? Because we continue to believe that we live in a meritocracy where those who do good get good and if someone is blessed it must be because he's earned it. And yet ...

Hosea, the righteous prophet, obeyed God by marrying the unloved, beloved, hardened sex worker, Gomer. He continued to call his profane nation to repentance, only to have his work come to nothing as the nation went off into exile. If we were living in a meritocracy, Hosea's work and words would have succeeded in producing the desired results, and he would have been rewarded for his faithfulness. *Do great things and you will be a success!* And yet ... Hosea never saw the fruit of his obedience. Where is the fairness in that?

That is simply the point. God isn't fair. At least, not in the ways we would like him to be. He is gracious and he refuses to order his world in ways that fit our self-promotion and self-salvation projects. But though we continue to misunderstand and tell others made-up fables about how they can earn their way into an Instagram-worthy life, we are still recipients of the Lord's love and grace.

Mary's Testimony

Now we come to our last story, about a young virgin who became pregnant outside marriage. Because of her faith, she should have been blessed with a great life, but instead her reputation was ruined (see John 8:41). She gave birth in a stable without a midwife or her mother to comfort her. She knew all along that the life of her dearly loved Son would eventually break her heart. Any expectation of blessing for obedience drained from her as she beheld his body hanging naked, shamed, and bleeding out on a Roman cross.

If anyone might have lived a life deserving of blessing, it was Mary. She spoke words of faith and boldly proclaimed the overthrow of all God's enemies.

> Oh, how my soul praises the Lord.
>> How my spirit rejoices in God my Savior!
> For he took notice of his lowly servant girl,
>> and from now on all generations will call
>>> me blessed.
> For the Mighty One is holy,
>> and he has done great things for me.
> He shows mercy from generation to generation
>> to all who fear him.
> His mighty arm has done tremendous things!
>> He has scattered the proud and haughty ones.
> He has brought down princes from their thrones
>> and exalted the humble.
> He has filled the hungry with good things
>> and sent the rich away with empty hands.
> He has helped his servant Israel
>> and remembered to be merciful.
> For he made this promise to our ancestors,
>> to Abraham and his children forever.
>
> (Luke 1:46–55 NLT)

Consider these beautiful words of faith. Mary is a theologian of the first order. The "lowly servant girl" will forever be called blessed. Mary was a denigrated nobody for whom the Mighty One did "great things." She gets it! She proclaimed the gospel before it was proclaimed by the mouth of the fetus still gestating in her uterus. And yet ... and yet. After she spoke these glorious words, the first hymn of the New Testament church, she received this heartbreaking prophecy about this baby she had paid so dearly for: "Indeed, this child is destined to cause the fall and rise of many in Israel and to be a sign that will be opposed—and a sword will pierce your own soul—that the thoughts of many hearts may be revealed" (Luke 2:34–35).

Your Son will be opposed and a sword will pierce your own soul. What mother could bear such a prophecy? Again, if there were anyone who should have been blessed for their great words of faith or their humble willingness to suffer for the Lord, it was Mary. And yet ...

Mary isn't the only faithful character who patiently suffered in this story. Her dear husband, Joseph, gave up his reputation and, in faith, took a woman who wasn't pure or undefiled in the eyes of his neighbors—as his bride. As a result of his doing so, his friends and neighbors thought perhaps he was the father after all. In their minds, the best-case scenario was that Mary had been raped by a Roman soldier and Joseph was just trying to cover for her. The worst case? She was a whore, and Joseph would have been right to, and in fact should have, divorced her and moved on to another, more worthy woman. And yet ... Joseph loved Mary and her child. He provided for them and taught Jesus to love and protect women and to walk in faith in the Lord, his true Father. Because he was a "righteous man," Joseph refused to publicly disgrace her. But he died before he saw even the beginning of the good news that this Son would bring. He faithfully obeyed the messenger who told him to love. And he died in faith before seeing the fulfillment of his hopes.

Getting It Right

It is part of the DNA of Americans to believe that a good life can be earned in a meritocracy. After all, we live in the land of promise where anyone (or so we're told) can make it big and live their dream. The lie is that, by working hard and silencing any negative thoughts, we can obtain the blessed life we long for. In other words, if we are diligent in our duties and believe that we are as wonderful as we've been told by parents, teachers, and Disney, then, as Tinkerbell says, "Every wish will come true." It's not hard to understand why secularists might believe such lies, but why do Christians, who know the truth, so often fall for this line of thinking? What biblical character, in any of these stories we've considered, proves that good works earn us a good life?

We have developed a peculiar form of pragmatic Christianity that works, or so we think. We have been told that the church needs to do a better job marketing a militant Jesus who will attract both men and women determined to do great things for God. And of course, it follows that our stellar reputation will then bring people to faith. And yet ...

We don't have any place for a theology that includes such people as the following:

- Hosea, an unsuccessful prophet, was committed to a lost cause.

- Abraham pimped out his wife to protect himself, slept with her slave, disbelieved the promise, and never received an abiding homeland.

- Sarah was unable to do the one thing her clan needed her to do, was abandoned by her brother-husband, was sexually abused by a foreign king, forced her slave into her husband's bed, and then abused her slave over and over again. And yet, she was given the son she longed for.

- Hagar, the nameless one with no rights, was disrespected and ran away from her master twice, assuming she'd die in the wilderness alone. And yet she had a shocking encounter with the Lord and is known as the matriarch of a nation.

- Judah, the jealous, wicked elder brother, sold Joseph into slavery, renounced his family, married a foreigner, raised two wicked sons whom God killed, lied to their widow, planned for her to live out her life in solitude and poverty, had sex with a prostitute, then wanted to burn his faithful daughter-in-law (and her unborn children) for the same thing. And yet he was given two sons and a place of honor among his brothers.

- Tamar, an unloved gentile and sexually abused wife, in faithfulness, humiliated herself so that she could raise sons for her wicked husband's name and courageously faced the condemnation of her wicked father-in-law. And yet, she found a place of protection and honor among God's people.

- Naomi, the blessed bitter woman, foolishly followed her foolish husband into Moab, where she lost him and her two sons but gained a faithful daughter-in-law whom she would never have imagined and didn't deserve. And yet she cuddled a blessed son on her lap as she found a home to rest in.

- Ruth didn't fit the mold of "biblical womanhood," the gentile woman who could heft eighty pounds of grain and propose marriage to a wealthy older man in the middle of the night after a party. And yet, her name is venerated among God's people even to this day.

- Boaz, the son of a notorious sex worker, thought married life was not something he could ever hope for. And yet, his story is told and retold as an example of an honorable man of courage and love.

- David, the bored, lustful voyeur, took another man's little lamb and had him killed to cover up his crime. And yet, he is known as a man who had a heart like God's.

- Bathsheba, the beautiful, faithful, and yet naive lamb, suffered sexual abuse at the hands of her husband's king, was widowed, and was bereaved of a baby, all within a few months. She has been wrongly held up in churches as an example of a seductress. And yet, she is listed in the genealogy of the longed-for Messiah.

- Joseph would have put his beloved betrothed, Mary, away without publicly shaming her, yet he chose to love and live a life of shame himself and never lived long enough to see even the beginning of his Son's ministry. And yet, his life of faithful courage and love is remembered every year by Christians across the globe.

- Mary believed the impossible, gave up everything, spoke words of faith, then questioned her Son's sanity, stood at the foot of the tree where her beloved was pinioned, bleeding out, forgiving his executioners, and questioning where his Father's smiling face had gone. And yet ... beloved, blessed Mary. She stands as the one who, like her Son after her, was willing to say, "Not my will but Thine be done."

Dear friends, this is who we are. These are our forefathers and mothers in the faith. And though it might seem like bad news, it is actually such good news for sinner-saints like us. In fact, it's the best news we could ever receive, because it means that our standing with the Lord doesn't depend on how well we do, how consistent our faith is, or how righteously we live. Everything depends on the grace of the Father, and the love of the Son, and the work of the Spirit. Nothing about salvation depends on you. And that is the most freeing news any of us will ever hear. Will you believe it?

The Chief of Sinners

Right about now you might be thinking: *No way, Elyse! I'm not any of those people! I've tried to live a good life, and I'm just not going to accept that reputation. I've worked hard and I know God sees all my effort, so I trust that I will be justly rewarded.*

Listen, I get that. I have worked for fifty-plus years to live a faithful Christian life and sometimes I forget grace. During those times, I hope that my labors mean I can expect good things for all my work. But when I recognize the shortfalls in my own life, faith, and love for God and neighbor, I am silenced. I know I deserve to flunk out of a meritocracy. And I'm not the only one.

At the end of his life—a life of faithful obedience and astonishing sacrifice—the apostle Paul had this testimony: "This saying is trustworthy and deserving of full acceptance: 'Christ Jesus came into the world to save sinners'—and I am the worst of them" (1 Timothy 1:15).

Can you say that with him? Can you say that Christ Jesus came into the world not to save the righteous who need no repentance (see Luke 5:32) but rather to save those who could never, would never, come to him in humility and plead for grace? Here is Paul's take on his life and the Lord's great grace: "But I received mercy *for this reason*, so that in me, the worst of them, Christ Jesus might demonstrate his extraordinary patience as an example to those who would believe in him for eternal life" (1 Timothy 1:16).

Have you received mercy? Why? Would you answer that question the way that Paul does? Have you received the kind of mercy that points to the "extraordinary patience" of Jesus? Yes, of course, our lives are meant to glorify God ... but do we glorify him by how strong and successful we are, or do we glorify him in our weakness? Do we tell our neighbors that God loves good people like us, or that he loves great sinners (like us) and that there's enough mercy for them there, too?

Can you see it? Paul and all of these dear brothers and sisters are just like you, just like me. Believing unbelievers. Obedient disobeyers. Faithful wafflers. Truthful deceivers. The confused, wandering, impatient waiters. And yet ...

Can you see it? We should all be called *unloved*, but instead we have been declared *beloved*. We are loved because he first loved us, because he *is* love. That is the most important thing about us: we are beloved of God. In fact, it's the only thing that will matter eternally. We are beloved *because he says we are*. Period.

So, let us put aside all the foolishness of the pragmatic, pull-yourself-up-by-your-own-bootstraps theology we have preached to ourselves all these years and instead throw ourselves on the grace of God. The same God who called and loved the unsuccessful Hoseas; the scheming, deceptive, and condemning Judahs; the disrespected Tamars; the abusive Abrahams, Sarahs, and Davids; the disillusioned and faithless Naomis; the outsiders like Ruth; the sons of whores like Boaz; the brokenhearted Bathshebas; and the maligned and suffering Josephs and Marys. Paul's testimony encourages me in this regard. He did great things, but that was not how he wanted to be remembered. He wanted to be remembered as the one who didn't deserve mercy, who was unloved—but who was, more importantly, crowned as beloved instead. Like them, we are all the unloved beloveds.

So, let's join the bedraggled, beloved saints before us and discover their joy by tearing down the meritocracy and instead walking straight into the life of shalom: of peace, joy, fullness, *in spite of all we see with our eyes, in spite of all we still want, in spite of the way we're denigrated or laughed at.* We are no longer unloved. Rather, now, and always, we are called *beloved*.

Digging Deeper

1. As you consider the lives of the people we've looked at, which stories most closely resonate with you? Why?

2. What would stop you from believing that God loves the imperfect kinds of people we have considered?

3. What would encourage you to believe that God loves these kinds of people?

4. In what ways have you fallen for the false theology of a meritocracy? How has that affected your life?

5. Do you believe that, even though your life might look like you're unloved, you are actually beloved? What are some truths you have learned throughout this book that will help remind you of this truth? List them.

6. Summarize what you've learned in this chapter in four or five sentences.

7. Summarize what you've learned in this book in four or five sentences.

Epilogue

I have never missed a deadline before. But with this book, I did. This book created a wrestling within me that eventuated in significant physical pain. It was difficult on a number of levels. First, I was depleted because I had just finished writing *Jesus and Gender* with Eric Schumacher, and the process pushed me to levels of thought and creativity that were far more challenging than I knew at the time. I have come to recognize that I have the ability to spin many plates at once, but I had never come to the end of my strength before. This time I did. Too many plates. Too many demands.

Why was I tempted to set myself up to fail in this way?

My mother died in November 2020, and my partially mentally disabled brother, whose care then fell on me, moved onto our property, only to have a series of significant strokes in the summer of 2021. This obligated me to deal with government social services while arranging for his ongoing care. I needed to arrange care for my brother, deal with my own autoimmune disease, record two podcasts a week, finish an eighty-thousand-word book, create a companion study guide, and write a script for video introductions to each chapter.

At the same time, I was the target of censure, primarily because I was seeking to champion the value of women from within ecclesiastical structures that assumed that anyone talking positively about women must be a (*gasp*) liberal feminist. The last three years have been difficult, to say the least, or what Brene Brown would call act 2: the messy, dark middle of my story.

In the midst of all this, I began this book. Conversations with friends and editors helped me along the way, but the root problem was that I was tired of writing books that were unloved and doing work that was only criticized. The truth is that I wasn't sure whether I was one of the beloved. I do hear, quite frequently, that my work has helped people, and many have been generous and kind in saying so. But in my heart I struggle to believe that I am ultimately lovable at my core. I can tell you, and have, over and over that the gospel says we are beloved, but I have to admit that sometimes I have trouble believing it myself. This book, about women and men whose lives were dumpster fires, is really a book about me. It's a book about the immense failures in my own life. The hypocrisy. Hatred. Pride. Lovelessness. The shame over who I am and how you might perceive me.

I'm Gomer, the beloved, who kept running back to her old way of life—at least in my heart. I'm Sarah, who couldn't fulfill the expectations placed on her and abused poor, vulnerable Hagar but still fulfilled God's plan in her old age. I'm Hagar, who met the Lord at that well in the desert and had to believe (more than once) that God saw and heard her. I'm Tamar, a who was intent on fulfilling God's will as a desperate widow and was declared righteous. I'm Naomi, who needed to be surprised by love as a bitter woman. I'm Ruth, who didn't fit into common tropes about femininity. I'm Bathsheba, who struggled with both wisdom and naivete, whose reputation was ruined. I'm Mary, who did believe and said yes, then had to watch the death of all her dreams.

And I'm just like you. I can say that I don't believe in the Negotiator God or the Gift Giver God. I can say that I don't believe that we live in a meritocracy and that everything is grace, but I still want to try to prove that I am worthy of acceptance. Sometimes I struggle to believe, and I know that a day is coming when that struggle will be over. I can't wait!

As you consider the course of your life, the way it speaks of either cursing or blessing, I hope you will stop to consider the good news that you are beloved by God. You don't need to negotiate with him, saying foolish things like, "I promise I will do thus-and-so, if you give me this." Children of loving fathers don't need to negotiate. They know they can simply ask him for what they truly need, and he will take care of them. Sometimes, out of his great love, even things they don't need will be granted to them.

I hope that, when you are tempted to see the Lord as a foolish old grandpa who gives too much sugar to children just to see them smile (and perhaps buy their love), you will instead rightly see him as the loving, wise King that he is. He is a good Father to his children. Most of all, I hope this book has helped you arrive at a place where you understand that the kingdom of God isn't a meritocracy. It's a kingdom where you are a citizen. That citizenship entitles you to all the blessings your Elder Brother has earned for you. You can't buy your citizenship in this kingdom; it's all a gift. And you can't earn your way up the royal ladder to try to get closer to the King. No, God the Father already holds you as close as the Son he loves.

Please don't misunderstand: you will still experience sorrow. Yes, sometimes your life will resemble the lives of those we have considered here. But their difficult lives weren't the finale of their story. They were only parts of a lifelong history, acts in the drama of their lives. Perhaps the answers you've been praying for will arrive tomorrow. Perhaps they won't arrive until you step into that glorious world to come. But they will arrive. Why? Because you who once thought of yourself as unloved are actually beloved. You are his. He is yours. This is all that matters. God's never-earned, freely given mercy is yours, in Christ, forever.

Acknowledgments

I'm so thankful for the women and men who have sought to free me from my incessant inner slavedriver and have taught me about the gospel of grace. Boy, do I need to hear it, and I mean *every day!* I'm thankful for my dear friends at Faithlife and Logos, especially for Scott Lindsey, Deb Keiser, and for the wonderful editing of Rachel Joy Welcher. I'm thankful for my pastors and their families at Grace Bible Church in Escondido, California, and for my dear family who continue to encourage and comfort me. I'm especially thankful for dear Phil who consoles me with pats and ice cream when I've got the "writing headache." And, of course, for all the people over the last half century who reminded me that Jesus was enough.

Appendix

How to Know You Are a Christian

I'm so glad that you turned to this appendix. If you are wondering what it means to be a Christian, I hope that this short explanation will help. If you think you are a Christian but just want to check to be sure, that's great, too! My prayer is that you will trust in Jesus and his work on the cross and that you will come to know how loved you are.

There really are only a few basic things you need to understand and believe.

- There is a good God who created all things, including me and you. We were made to be like him and trust in him (that is called "holiness").

- We have failed to be like him or trust him. Instead we trust in ourselves (that is called "sin").

- We need God's help to be like him. He has provided all the help we need in Jesus Christ (that is called the "good news" or "gospel"). At its core, the gospel is simply the news about what Jesus did for us: he died in our place, taking the punishment for our sin, and then he rose from the dead, proving that his work was sufficient to save us.

- We have to believe the gospel and accept the help that Jesus has given. We do that by trusting in him and not in ourselves (that is called "faith").

Okay, that's about it. Really basic, right?

What you have heard about Christianity might not have been quite so simple, though. Over the two thousand years since Jesus lived, billions (trillions?) of words have been spoken and written about all the above. An untold number of people have believed some form of this really basic message and have added depth and nuance that have made Christianity rich with meaning and beauty. Sometimes that makes our faith seem complicated, but it really isn't. In fact, even little children can understand it. Let's look at each of the points above more closely.

- There is a good God who created all things, including me and you. We were made to be like him and trust in him (that is called "holiness").

The Bible tells us that God made the world and everything in it (Genesis 1–2; Acts 17:24). What that means is that God existed before anything was, and out of his love he chose to make all there is, including all people. Because he made everything, he has the right to tell us how to live. He wants us to live holy lives. That doesn't mean that we walk around with pinched faces all the time. What it means is that we love people and live in ways that honor them and the God who made us all. But not only that; he also knows the kind of life that will make us happiest. His right way is a way of love: love for him and love for our neighbor. Doesn't that sound like a beautiful way to live?

- We have failed to be like him or trust him. Instead we trust in ourselves (that is called "sin").

Sadly, from nearly the very beginning of time, people have chosen to live for themselves. Instead of loving their neighbor or trusting that God's way is best, they mistreat and hate their neighbor and try to make themselves happy on their own (see Titus 3:3). This has resulted in terrible conflict, pain, and destruction. Instead of happily enjoying all the good gifts God has given, they have turned their backs on God and tried to earn their way to happiness through their own plans and works. They have consistently failed, no matter how hard they've tried. This is the reason for all the tears that are shed in the world. Thankfully, God has not left us alone in this mess, even though we might have wanted him to. He made a way for us out of our sin.

- We need his help to be like him. God has provided all the help we need in Jesus Christ (that is called the "good news" or "gospel").

Instead of leaving us alone in our sad mess, God sent his Son to us. This Son was born as a regular baby (what we celebrate at Christmas) and lived a life of perfect holiness. His name was Jesus, the Messiah (or Christ). He always loved his Father and his neighbor (see John 8:29). He always trusted his Father's will, even when it was difficult (see Matthew 26:39). He did everything we should have done. Because it isn't right for people who haven't loved God or others to receive the blessings that obedience brings, Jesus also took the punishment we deserve for us. Although he was executed by Roman overlords, he was actually fulfilling his Father's plan to bring forgiveness to us (see Acts 4:27–28). He took the punishment our lovelessness and disobedience earned. We get the blessing he gained through his obedience. Then, three days after Jesus died, his Father raised him from the dead (see 1 Corinthians 15:3–5), proving that he had perfectly accomplished all the work he had been sent to do (what we celebrate at Easter). Then, Jesus met with his followers for forty days after his resurrection and finally ascended into heaven. Someday he will return, take all his people to himself, and remake the whole world into what it should have been: a place of peace and deep love for God and others ... forever (see 1 Corinthians 15:50–57). This is the good news (that's what the word "gospel" means): Jesus did everything that needed to be done so that you can be free from your struggle with sin and live with him forever.

- We have to believe the gospel and accept the help that Jesus has given. We do that by trusting in him and not in ourselves (that is called "faith").

Faith simply means that we stop trusting in ourselves, in our own ability to be good enough or work hard enough to earn a happy or blessed life. It means that we transfer our trust to God, who has promised to love us and give us all we need in this life and to resurrect us to eternal life with him after we die. None of us ever does this perfectly or even consistently. But if, at the end of the day, you can say, "Jesus, I'm trusting that you have forgiven my sins because I've asked and that you'll help me live a life of love," then you can rely on his promise to answer your prayer. If you'd like to pray something like that now, you can. Just ask God to forgive you for failing to love him and others, then ask him to help you follow him. Yes, it's that easy. And that's the point: you don't have to work to earn God's favor. It's a free gift (see Romans 6:23).

A Few More Thoughts

Since the Lord knows that it's difficult to walk this life of faith when we don't understand everything and can't see him, he has given us help. The first and greatest help is the work of the Holy Spirit. The Spirit opens our eyes to see, believe, and grow in our understanding of the truth about who Jesus is, what he has done, and how we should respond. He does this primarily through the Bible. The Bible helps us know God's thoughts and gives us direction on how to live. Personally, I use the Christian Standard Bible, but you can use any version of the Bible that you like. I recommend that you start reading in the New Testament, maybe in the book of Matthew, which narrates the story of the life of Jesus Christ. Before you read, ask the Holy Spirit to help you understand what you need to know.

Second, since the Spirit will speak to us through others, I would urge you to find a community of Christians you can learn from and with. If there are churches where you live, you can see whether they are good by reading what is usually called a statement of faith on their website. If they talk about Jesus being the only way to God, then they're probably a good place for you. If they talk about anything else you need to do to be saved aside from trusting in what Jesus has already done, you might want to avoid them.

Finally, we can trust that the Lord will hear us when we pray, so let me encourage you to live a life of prayer. You don't have to say any special words. Your Father, who loves you, will hear you and answer your prayer in the best way: his way. There are also free prayer apps for your phone. I use the Lectio 365 app daily and love the way it pushes me outside my routine way of praying the same thing over and over.

I hope that this very brief explanation of Christianity is helpful for you. If you have decided to trust in Jesus and his work for you, please write to me at the publisher and tell me all about it. I would love to hear from you.

Endnotes

1. Duane A. Garrett, Hosea, *Joel: An Exegetical and Theological Exposition of Holy Scripture*, New American Commentary (Nashville: Broadman & Holman, 1997), 94.
2. Leonard J. Coppes, "2028 קָלַל," ed. R. Laird Harris, Gleason L. Archer Jr., and Bruce K. Waltke, *Theological Wordbook of the Old Testament* (Chicago: Moody Press, 1999), 800.
3. Carolyn Custis James, *Lost Women of the Bible* (Grand Rapids: Zondervan, 2005), 93.
4. Bruce K. Waltke with Cathi J. Fredricks, *Genesis: A Commentary* (Grand Rapids: Zondervan, 2001), 513.
5. David D. Pettus, "Tamar," in *Lexham Bible Dictionary*, ed. John D. Barry et al. (Bellingham, WA: Lexham, 2012).
6. Pgs. 68-69: Douglas Mangum, Miles Custis, and Wendy Widder, *Genesis 12-50*, Lexham Research Commentaries (Bellingham, WA: Lexham Press, 2013), Gen 38:1-30.
7. Waltke, *Genesis*, 515.
8. Nahum M. Sarna, *The JPS Torah Commentary: Genesis* (Philadelphia: Jewish Publication Society of America, 2001), 268.
9. Charles L. Feinberg, "117 אָמַץ," ed. R. Laird Harris, Gleason L. Archer Jr., and Bruce K. Waltke, *Theological Wordbook of the Old Testament* (Chicago: Moody Press, 1999), 53.
10. Iain M. Duguid, *Esther and Ruth*, ed. Richard D. Phillips and Philip Graham Ryken, Reformed Expository Commentary (Phillipsburg, NJ: P&R Publishing, 2005), 142-43.
11. Duguid, *Esther and Ruth*, 124.
12. John D. Barry et al., *Faithlife Study Bible* (Bellingham, WA: Lexham Press, 2012, 2016), 396.
13. Duguid, *Esther and Ruth*, 136.
14. Duguid, *Esther and Ruth*, 138.

15. "Infidelity Rates by Country 2023," World Population Review, https://worldpopulationreview.com/country-rankings/infidelity-rates-by-country.

16. Richard D. Phillips, *2 Samuel*, Reformed Expository Commentary (Phillipsburg, NJ: P&R, 2018), 206.

17. John R. Bisagno, *Principle Preaching: How to Create and Deliver Purpose Driven Sermons for Life Applications* (Nashville: Broadman & Holman, 2002), 95.

18. Scott L. Tatum, "2 Samuel," in *The Teacher's Bible Commentary*, ed. H. Franklin Paschall and Herschel H. Hobbs (Nashville: Broadman and Holman Publishers, 1972), 184.

19. Richard R. Losch, *All the People in the Bible: An A–Z Guide to the Saints, Scoundrels, and Other Characters in Scripture* (Grand Rapids: Eerdmans, 2008), 59.

20. Herbert M. Wolf, "1–2 Samuel," in *Evangelical Commentary on the Bible*, vol. 3, Baker Reference Library (Grand Rapids: Baker Books, 1995), 219.

21. Losch, *All the People in the Bible*, 95, 433.

22. 1124 לָקַח (*lāqaḥ*) take (get, fetch), lay hold of (seize), receive, acquire (buy), bring, marry (take a wife), snatch (take away). Walter C. Kaiser, "1124 לָקַח," ed. R. Laird Harris, Gleason L. Archer Jr., and Waltke, *Theological Wordbook*, 481.

23. James E. Smith, *The Books of History* (Joplin, MO: College Press, 1995), 354.

24. Phil Ryken, *When Trouble Comes* (Wheaton, IL: Crossway, 2016), 638.

25. David L. Turner and Darrell L. Bock, *Matthew, Mark,* Cornerstone Biblical Commentary (Carol Stream, IL: Tyndale House, 2006), 37.

26. Caring Well Report, https://caringwell.com/wp-content/uploads/2019/06/SBC-Caring-Well-Report-June-2019.pdf.

Bibliography

Bisagno, John R. *Principle Preaching: How to Create and Deliver Purpose Driven Sermons for Life Applications*. Nashville: Broadman & Holman, 2002.

Duguid, Iain M. *Esther and Ruth*. Reformed Expository Commentary. Phillipsburg, NJ: P&R, 2005.

Garrett, Duane A. *Hosea, Joel: An Exegetical and Theological Exposition of Holy Scripture*. New American Commentary. Nashville: Broadman & Holman, 1997.

James, Carolyn Custis. *Lost Women of the Bible*. Grand Rapids: Zondervan, 2005.

Losch, Richard R. *All the People in the Bible: An A–Z Guide to the Saints, Scoundrels, and Other Characters in Scripture*. Grand Rapids: Eerdmans, 2008.

Pettus, David D. "Tamar." In *Lexham Bible Dictionary*, ed. John D. Barry et al. Bellingham, WA: Lexham, 2012.

Phillips, Richard D. *2 Samuel*. Reformed Expository Commentary. Phillipsburg, NJ: P&R, 2018.

Ryken, Phil. *When Trouble Comes*. Wheaton, IL: Crossway, 2016.

Sarna, Nahum M. *The JPS Torah Commentary: Genesis*. Philadelphia: Jewish Publication Society of America, 2001.

Smith, James E. *The Books of History*. Joplin, MO: College Press, 1995.

Turner, David L., and Darrell L. Bock. *Matthew, Mark*. Cornerstone Biblical Commentary. Carol Stream, IL: Tyndale House, 2006.

Waltke, Bruce K., with Cathi J. Fredricks. *Genesis: A Commentary*. Grand Rapids: Zondervan, 2001.

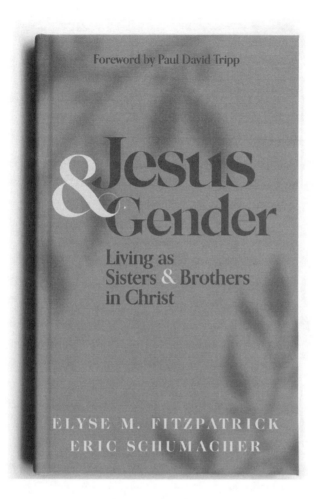

ALSO AVAILABLE

In *Jesus and Gender*, Elyse Fitzpatrick and Eric Schumacher explore how the life and way of Jesus offers a better path forward in Christian conversations about gender.

Visit lexhampress.com/jesus-and-gender